The Deep South Natural Foods Cookbook

The Deep South Natural Foods Cookbook

Mary Lou McCracken

Illustrated by Laurin McCracken

Stackpole Books

THE DEEP SOUTH NATURAL FOODS COOKBOOK

Copyright © 1975 by Mary Lou McCracken

Published by
STACKPOLE BOOKS
Cameron and Kelker Streets
Harrisburg, Pa. 17105

This hardcover edition published by special arrangement with Pyramid Communications, Inc.

Printed in the U.S.A.

Library of Congress Cataloging in Publication Data

McCracken, Mary Lou, 1943-
  The Deep South natural foods cookbook.

    Bibliography: p.
    Includes index.
    1. Cookery, American—Southern States. I. Title.
TX715.M134   641.5'975   75-6698
ISBN 0-8117-0491-2

To the memory of J. D. Oswalt who loved the South
and its food

Welcome to the Deep South, a pleasant place where flowers grow the year around. The magnolia blossoms are the color of ivory with deeply carved leaves. The summer evenings are heavily filled with the scent of honeysuckle. There is the contrast of the mansion and the poor farm dwellings. The South is composed of many things that seem stark in contrast, but in combination make the South an unforgetable place. Regardless of their economic level, the people share a common pride, traditional beliefs and values, and a genuine hospitality.

CONTENTS

INTRODUCTION

Nothing is as well liked by all my family members as good, natural Southern home cooking. These recipes have their origins in the plantation days gone by before the existence of artificial preservatives and additives. On the market today are various pseudonatural foods cookbooks hastily written in an effort to cash in on the homemaker's new interest in more nutritional foods for her family. I too have become concerned about the additives in the foods that I prepare for my family. This concern has led me to take a new look at products on the supermarket shelves and to *read the labels* more carefully. I find myself buying less and less at the supermarket, turning instead to the shelves of my local nutrition center. All of this has caused me to turn back to my Southern recipes when planning my menus. Most authenic Southern recipes need little revision to fit today's natural foods criteria. Where revision is needed I have substituted after careful testing in my own kitchen. Traditional Southern cooking is honest cooking with a minimum of fancy ingredients. The emphasis is on basic vegetables, fruits, meats, and grains. Even the vegetarian would find that by omitting the meats the remaining chapters would supply a satisfying and nutritious diet.

To better understand the cooking of the South one would enjoy reading of its heritage. Settlers came to the South from many European countries to conquer a country almost bursting with fertility. It was through the West Indies and the Southern states that Europeans were first introduced to North America and its strange foods. The Southern Indians were excellent cooks. They made substantial contributions to today's Southern diet. Women of the Cherokee, Choctaw, Seminole, Powhatan, Creek, and other tribes developed hundreds of recipes. Many of these such as Brunswick stew, corn pone, hominy and hominy grits, roasted peanuts, and fried green tomatoes are still favorites today. The Southern women and their black cooks adapted the native foods and varied them in some cases, but the Southern Indian's creative additions to the Southerner's diet remain mostly unchanged today. Black mammies rarely bothered to write down their recipes since few could read or write. But recipes gathered from crumbling old notebooks and family recipe files undoubtedly in many cases owe their origin to the mammies. A ditty from an old unknown source expresses the talent of the mammies:

> *Just put 'em in front of*
> *an old wooded stove with*
> *the fixin's and they created somethin'*
> *grand special!*

2

Ultimately the English settled most of the land, but the Gallic and Hispanic areas maintained much of their separate identities, all of which is reflected in the cooking of the South. Harnett Kane tells of the Yankee husband who was watching his Mississippi Delta wife in the kitchen as she tried to prepare a New England dinner which he remembered from his childhood. "She cut the vegetables, she washed them, she put them in the pot; and she added tomatoes, bay leaf, thyme, onions, and five or six other items without which she was sure no dish was complete. The husband, grinning told her: 'Bebe, no matter what you put on that stove, it's going to come out French—your own kind of French.' "[1]

The emphasis of the English settlers was on setting up the countryside as they remembered it. Gradually large cities developed, but the tradition of the country was dominated by families fond of superb food and parties. Genuine good-humored hospitality survived and remains unequaled by any other region. In the folkways of Southern gastronomy, eating and drinking have played great roles in hospitality and sociability. The needs of religion, work, and politics are satisfied in the community gatherings such as harvest suppers, church picnics, cornhuskings, butchering day dinners, all day sings, barbecues, fish fries, and oyster roasts. Around the regional dishes of the South have grown up family recipes, local traditions, and legends. Of all ethnic influences in the South none are more subtly pervasive than those of food and diet.

Fine cooking and gracious dining are as much a part of the South as colonnaded plantation homes. After the Civil War the Southern tradition became very important as the proud people began to glamorize the past. The Southern way of life is a state of mind, an emotional attachment that endures in its food. The "take-your-time, sit-down-and-enjoy-yourself" philosophy makes life more pleasurable.

There are large variations as you travel from one region to another. But internal variations are minor as compared with the differences between Southerners and people from

[1] Kane, Harnett, *Deep Delta Country*, page 77.

3

other areas of the country. They all share a common heritage that they cling to. William Faulkner once wrote, "You can't understand it. You would have to be born there."[2] Born there or not, anyone can enjoy these recipes that for over 300 years have come from the fires of camping settlers, the iron pot hanging over the cabin fireplaces, the brick kitchens behind the main house, and from the mammy in the slave cabin.

[2] *Ibid.*

GLOSSARY OF INGREDIENTS

LEARN TO READ LABELS. You'll be surprised how many things that you wouldn't care to eat are in your processed foods.

ARROWROOT—A flour made from the roots of the cassava plant which may be substituted for cornstarch or flour for thickening. 4 tablespoons arrowroot = 3 tablespoons cornstarch. 1 tablespoon flour = 1 teaspoon arrowroot.

BAKING POWDER—Look at the label and choose one that is aluminum free. Walnut Acres sells a natural double–acting aluminum free baking powder. Most natural food cooks believe that aluminum is a health hazard although the case has yet to be proven against aluminum.

BAKING SODA—Some strict health food cooks will not use this in their foods because they say it neutralizes the stomach acids, thereby destroying food values, so I don't put it in cooked vegetables or casseroles. However, it may be used in the recipes given here as it is used to neutralize the acidity of buttermilk. Baking soda is available in my health food store.

BREWER'S YEAST—This is dried yeast which does not have leavening powers, but is extremely rich in the B complex vitamins. It is also a rich, inexpensive source of complete protein. It can be mixed into fruit or vegetable juices.

BUTTER—This is the most palatable of all the fats and is easily digested. Its role in the formation of cholesterol is still controversial. I like to use it in moderation. (See SOY MARGARINE)

5

CAROB POWDER—This health food substitute for chocolate is made from the dried pulp of carob pods (St. John's bread) and is suited for confections, hot or cold milk drinks, cakes, icings, cookies, fudge, and syrups. There is even a substitute for chocolate chips called caro-coa nuggets. Carob powder is alkaline, high in calcium, rich in natural sugars, low in starch, and low in fats. It has 2% fat as compared with 25% fat in chocolate. It is sold in powder form and also sweetened and pressed into bars. 3 tablespoons carob powder plus 2 tablespoons water = 1 square chocolate.

CAST IRON COOKWARE—The favorite cookware of the Southern cook. It is uncoated natural cast iron that with use developes a black crust all over. It is sold in hardware and department stores. Don't be fooled by its light gray surface as was the young bride that my daddy loved to tell about. She wanted to buy some cookware like her mother used, but told him that she could not find any black cookware, only the gray pans.

CHICKEN—As for meats, buy your chicken if possible where you know the conditions under which it has been raised. I buy chicken only at my local health food store after reading about the treatment of the creatures in *Meat Eaters Are Threatened* (see bibliography). Be sure that the poultry you buy has not been given stilbestrol which is used to induce quick weight gain. Antibiotics are also used to keep poultry alive in unnatural environments which is unhealthful as well as inhumane. Chicken and turkey have a slightly higher protein content than beef, veal and considerably higher protein content than pork or lamb. Health food stores carry meats and poultry which have been raised on organic feed and under humane conditions.

CHEESE—Buy only the cheeses labeled as aged, natural cheeses made without preservatives and artificial coloring. These can be obtained in some supermarkets, at most health food stores, or can be shipped to you from various suppliers during the cool months.

COCONUT—Use grated or powdered coconut meal from the health food store or prepare your own. A coconut freshly prepared at home is better in flavor than any other, however. Prepare it as follows: With an ice pick or nails hammered in, make holes in the eyes of the coconut. Drain the milk out. Save milk for flavoring drinks or desserts. Put the coconut into a 350 degree F. oven for about 30 minutes. Tap all over with the hammer. Then break open. Pry out the meat and peel the dark skin off with a sharp little knife. Then grate the coconut and use according to the recipe. Store in a tightly closed container in the refrigerator. Coconut is a good natural sweetener for desserts, cereals, bread and cake products.

CORN GRITS—I use white hominy grits.

CORN MEALS—Try to find the stone ground, unfumigated brands. You will find it packaged in yellow and white meals. I use yellow. Walnut Acres sells corn meals.

CRACKERS—There are crackers and wafers available in the health food stores and some supermarkets now which contain all natural ingredients.

EGGS—If available, use fertile eggs from happy chickens that are allowed to roam, scratch, and mate. Chickens should not be injected with hormones and should be fed organic feed free from insecticides.

FLOUR—I buy and use absolutely no white flour unless it is labeled "unbleached." Bleached flour has been whitened with chlorine which has caused stunted growth in test animals.[3] Unbleached flours are now available in most supermarkets, but if for some reason you absolutely must use one of the bleached flours at least make up its nutritional lacks even though you can't change the effects of the use of chlorine. Cornell University makes the following suggestion for enriching your own flour: for each cup of bleached flour first put into the measuring cup 1 teaspoon wheat germ, 1 tablespoon soy flour, and 1 tablespoon non-instant

[3] Levitt, Eleanor, *The Wonderful World of Natural Food Cookery,* p. 18.

dry milk. Then fill the cup the rest of the way with the bleached flour. Do this before adding each cup to the recipe. When a recipe calls for unbleached flour you may use half unbleached flour and half whole wheat except when a white product is desired. El Molina Mills packages a large variety of organic flours and meals. Heckers packages an unbleached flour available in the supermarket.

HONEY—The honey in the supermarket is often marked 100% pure. However, the commercial process of high heat and filtering can destroy some of the food value and the enzymes, including the natural pollen which people with allergies like to have in their honey. Therefore I prefer to buy organic unfiltered honey from the health food stores or from a local bee keeper where it is cheaper. You can choose from clover, thyme, basswood, sage, buckwheat, orange blossom and others. Try small jars of different ones to find your favorites. Usually the darker the honey, the stronger the flavor. The use of honey is certainly more beneficial than the use of refined sugar and I have included honey in many recipes. I buy a local wild flower honey or the safflower honey from the nutrition center. Natural honey can be substituted for sugar using 1 cup honey for 1 cup sugar and reducing the liquid in the recipe by 1/4 cup.

MEATS—Meat should be obtained from a local meat producer if possible. If you are unsure of your beef products your health food store may have organically grown meat available frozen. Mine has roasts, ground beef and sirloin, cubed beef, and steaks, all organically grown and free of any additives. Shiloh Farms has delicious hot dogs and sausage made from beef that taste like pork but contain none. They also package several lunch meats that are very good and again contain no nitrites or other preservatives with which supermarket brands of cold cuts are loaded.

MILK—I use whole, pasteurized milk. You may prefer to use raw milk from certified cows if it is available. Ask your local health food store. Pasteurization alters the biochemistry of milk, which includes the protein and minerals, making them less available or not available at all. Pasteurized milk does not keep as long as certified raw milk because pasteurization destroys the friendly acid-forming bacteria which fight off the growth of invading bacteria which cause spoilage. Non-instant skimmed milk is available in the health food stores. It is not as instant mixing as the regular instant milk. 2/3 cup of non-instant milk contains 35 grams of complete protein as compared with 2/3 cup regular instant milk which contains 18 grams of complete protein.

MOLASSES—Molasses is used a lot in Southern cooking. The darker the molasses, the better. Light-colored molasses shows that it has been refined and bleached. Barbados is one type of unbleached molasses which is quite high in minerals and vitamins. Blackstrap, the residue of refined white sugar, is, as its name implies, a dark variety, high in potassium, calcium, and iron. Compare this with refined white sugar for nutrition! Sorghum syrup is also used which is a dark, heavy molasses-like syrup made from a cane-like grass. If this is used I use half sorghum and half molasses. Dr. J. Sim Wallace says in *Oral Hygiene* that "Sugar is so highly refined that we may almost say that it is not a food but a pure chemical product produced in quantity for the destruction of the teeth."[4]

NUTS—Peanuts and pecans are the two nuts used most often in Southern cooking. If you are lucky enough to have your own pecan tree or a neighbor with one, your problem is solved. If you must, buy them in the supermarket, but buy the ones still in their shells so you can be sure no chemicals have been added to extend their shelf life. Shelled pecans freeze well and last for as long as two years. Of course, if you buy nuts from your health food store they will be labeled as organic and free from additives.

PORK AND HAM—Southerners use a lot of pork and ham in their cooking. Some object to the use of pork products, thinking them unfit for human consumption

---

[4] Quoted in *About Molasses,* Pyramid, p. 17.

because of the use of the chemical curing agents or for Biblical reasons. If you share these feelings, there is a product WHAM on the market manufactured by Worthington Foods, Inc., Worthington, Ohio 43085, a subsidiary of Miles Laboratories, Inc. WHAM comes frozen in slices, in a ham roll, or canned. It smells and tastes like ham, but is made of soy protein. It is precooked, rich in protein, low in fat, and low in calories. This same company makes chicken slices from soy protein that are delicious. If you do not object to the use of pork in your diet you could buy pork, keeping in mind the same criteria as for beef and poultry. Again let me mention Shiloh Farms, producers of hot dogs, cold cuts, and sausages that taste as if they contain pork, but are all organic beef, not a bit of pork.

RAISINS—Buy untreated and unsulfured raisins and other dried fruits such as dates, apples, and figs from the health food store. I have recently seen the unsulfured fruits in a local supermarket. The regular supermarket dried fruit packages state that they contain sulfur dioxide. Read the labels. Many honey-dipped dried fruits are available in the health food stores.

RICE—Use brown rice. My favorite brand available in the supermarket is Riviana. Only the outer husk has been removed from natural brown rice. Sometimes I combine equal parts brown rice and wild rice.

OATS—Use rolled oats, meal, or flour. They should be labeled "steel cut."

OILS—Southern cooking traditionally contains large amounts of animal fats. These recipes use only vegetable oils such as peanut, sesame, safflower, and sunflower. Whichever vegetable oil you prefer to use it should be labeled "cold-pressed, no additives." In some recipes I prefer to use butter, but there is the choice of butter or soy margarine.

SALT—Use natural sea salt that contains iodine. Vegetable salt, which is iodized salt mixed with dried vegetables is also very good, but most of the time I use the sea salt.

SOY FLOUR or SOY POWDER—Available in health food stores. It is packaged full fat or low fat. 1 cup = 60 grams complete protein.

SEAFOOD—Seafood should be obtained locally from a fish market where you know the sources of the fish. In choosing fresh fish the flesh should be firm and should not have a strong fishy or foul odor. Don't be embarrassed to smell the fish before it is wrapped. Frozen and canned fish products are available in health food stores.

SOY MARGARINE—If you had rather not use butter you may substitute a margarine made from soy, sesame, safflower, or wheat germ oils. I like the soy bean spread "Willow Run" made by Shedd-Bartush Foods, Division of Beatrice Foods Co., Detroit, Michigan 48238.

SUGAR—Raw sugar or unrefined brown sugar is preferred to the white refined sugar which should be avoided. When the recipe calls for pulverized raw sugar put the sugar into the blender for a few seconds until it is finer and less grainy.

WHEAT GERM—Available fresh, raw or toasted. Also now available sugared and flavored. I use the plain toasted.

YEAST—I use dry granular yeast with no preservatives. Available in some supermarkets and all health food stores.

Dixie Breads, Dressings and Grits

Before De Soto discovered the Mississippi River the Chickasaw Indians along the Natchez Trace had already cultivated fields of corn. Their chiefs went to De Soto with gifts of corn and game. In the South today people eat significant quantities of field corn, a staple grain.

"Bread" to a Southerner means corn bread. The corn used may be bought either smoothly ground or taken to a local mill and coarsely ground which gives a more satisfying taste and texture. There is a wide variation in cornbreads ranging from the hoe cake of slavery and Civil War times, when soldiers baked it on their bayonets before the fires, to the soft melt–in–your–mouth spoon bread.

Some of the whole corn kernels are leached with lye and made into hominy, a process developed by the Southern Indians. Hominy may be eaten whole as a vegetable or may be dried and ground into small particles which are then called hominy grits. Boiled hominy grits are still a standard breakfast dish in most Southern homes. They appear on tables back home as often as potatoes in other parts of the country. They are good served at any meal with fried fish, scrambled eggs, or with a poached egg on top of a heap of hot grits.

Hot rolls, biscuits, or corn bread are considered a necessity with each meal. The Southern hot bread had a frontier origin. When wheat came in, its most obvious use was in the preparation of biscuits, the successor to hot hoe cakes.

The slave cooks found another use for corn bread taken from their African heritage. This was the breaded preparation placed inside and about a chicken or turkey when baked. Today it is called "dressing." In the Old South the word "cush" was used for this preparation of corn bread, chopped-up onions, celery, salt, and pepper. Evidence

12

shows that the word "cush" was brought by slaves from Africa where the term *kushkush* prevails in some dialects, meaning a thin cake of wheaten flour, ground nuts, or parched meal. Further investigation shows that the word was not native with the Africans, however. It was passed from Arabic into one or another of the African dialects. Arabs used the word *couscous* to mean flour mixed with small amounts of water until small grain-like particles were formed. From the Arabs it also found its way into the French language. The first actual evidence of the use of a similar word in the South occurs in 1770 in Maryland. Spelled *cushie*, it meant a pancake made of Indian corn. There its immediate source was the Dutch people in whose language it is spelled *koeskoes,* meaning a mixture of different kinds of meat and greens.

Another exclusive Southern bread preparation is the "hush puppy" which is usually served informally in the home when one is frying fresh-caught fish. The tradition of the hush puppy goes back to the hunt and the fishing trip. They say that the name for this bread came from the times when the hunters sat around the camp fire eating heartily as the Negro cooks prepared the food. The hunting dogs whined for the men's food as they tugged at their leashes. The cook or huntsman would toss the left-over little corn patties to the dogs calling "Hush, puppies!"

The breads in this chapter will bring a new taste, smell, and sight to your table. No other form of cooking is so simple yet gives as much satisfaction as the making of breads.

Corn Pone

Pones are flattened cakes of corn meal and water. They were the basic everyday bread of the Southern Indians. This is said to be the first corn bread baked by the colonists in Virginia in the early 1600's. By observing the Indian cooks, the colonists learned to make the Indian bread their way by pounding the kernels in a mortar to make a fine meal. The Indians usually baked the bread on wooden paddles or tossed the cakes in hot coals, hence the English name "ashcakes" for the little patties that are now commonly called "pones."

2   cups stone ground yellow corn meal
1   teaspoon sea salt
1/8 teaspoon baking soda
     water

Sift the dry ingredients together. Add just enough water to the dry ingredients to hold them together. Shape into pones by patting the mixture in the palms of your hands into little cakes or patties. Bake in a 400 degrees F. oven until a brown crust has formed, about 25–30 minutes.

Makes 10 pones

Hoe Cake

This very primitive bread with a sweet and nutty flavor and satisfying texture is a good accompaniment for sausage or ham at breakfast. It is also tasty served with butter and Southern molasses or honey. The ingredients are similar to those contained in CORN PONE, but it is cooked differently. From accounts of Southern slaves this is the bread that they took to the fields with them.

1 cup stone ground yellow corn meal
1/2 teaspoon sea salt
boiling water

Mix salt and corn meal. Pour into it and stir constantly enough boiling water to make a batter that does not spread when placed on the griddle. Heat an iron griddle or iron skillet until hot. Grease with oil. Spread batter in one large cake about 1/2" thick. Cook slowly, turning when well browned. Brown the other side.

Serves 4

Corn Bread Sticks

2   cups stone ground yellow corn meal
3/4   teaspoon baking soda
3/4   teaspoon sea salt
1   fertile egg
1½ to 2 cups buttermilk
3   tablespoons melted bacon fat or butter or cold-pressed
     oil

Sift together the meal, baking soda and salt. Combine the egg, milk, and fat or oil. Add to the dry ingredients. Stir just enough to moisten. Mixture will be rough. Fill *hot* oiled cast iron stick pan molds each about 2/3 full. Bake in 400 degrees F. oven for 25 minutes or until the sticks are golden brown. Turn the corn sticks out of the pan. Arrange on a hot platter and serve at once.

Makes 14 corn sticks

The same recipe may be used to make corn bread muffins or skillet bread. For muffins pour the batter into a hot greased muffin tin and for skillet bread pour the batter into a heavy cast iron skillet. Cook the muffins in a 400 degrees F. oven

16

25–30 minutes or until golden. Bake the skillet bread in a 400 degrees F. oven about 45 minutes or until the corn-bread begins to draw away from the edges of the skillet and the top is a rich golden brown. Cut the skillet bread into wedge-shaped pieces and serve from the skillet or unmold and place on a hot platter for serving.

Makes 12 muffins or
1 making of skillet bread

Johnny Cake

This is Yankee-style corn bread sweetened a bit with a little flour added.

1½   cups stone ground corn meal
1   cup unbleached flour
1/3   cup pulverized raw sugar
1   teaspoon sea salt
1   tablespoon baking powder
2   fertile eggs
6   tablespoons melted butter or margarine
1½   cups milk

Sift the dry ingredients together. Add the other ingredients to the dry ingredients in the order listed. Mix together. Batter will be a little rough. Cook the same as CORN BREAD STICKS, MUFFINS, and SKILLET BREAD, page 16. Servings are about the same.

Crackling Bread

This is an interesting variation on corn bread using cracklings, the crisp rind of roasted pork. If you cannot purchase cracklings ready to use, make them yourself.

Use the basic corn bread recipe. Place 1/4 lb. of finely chopped salt pork or fat back over moderate heat, stirring frequently until the bits are crisp and brown and have rendered all their fat. Remove and drain the pork bits. These are the cracklings. (Instead of the cracklings you could use chopped up bits of WHAM for a ham-like taste in your corn bread.) Stir into the corn bread mixture. Discard the fat. Pour the batter into a hot greased skillet. Bake in a 400 degrees F. oven for 35–45 minutes or until golden brown and the bread begins to draw away from the edges of the skillet. Cut the crackling bread into wedge pieces and serve from the skillet or unmold and place on a hot platter for serving.

Serves 6–8

Southern Spoon Bread

Spoon bread resembles a soufflé as it is served straight from the dish after it is well puffed and browned on top.

4   cups milk
1   cup stone ground yellow corn meal
2   tablespoons butter or soy margarine
1¾   teaspoons sea salt
4   fertile eggs

Scald the milk in a double boiler. Add corn meal and cook to a thin mush, about 5 minutes. Add butter and salt. Separate the eggs and beat the yolks. Beat the egg whites until stiff and then fold them into the corn meal mixture. Pour into a greased 1½ quart casserole and bake in a hot preheated 400 degrees F. oven 45 minutes or until well puffed and browned on top. Serve by the spoonful directly from the dish and top with butter or margarine.

Serves 6

Corn Bread Dressing

This is the basic Southern dressing. Some people would omit the dry bread crumbs and use corn bread exclusively. Try this and I don't think you'll ever again be satisfied with a prepackaged mix.

4   cups crumbled corn bread
2   cups dry bread crumbs
3½   cups chicken stock
3   fertile eggs
1   cup milk
2   teaspoons sea salt
1/2   teaspoon freshly ground pepper
1   cup finely chopped celery
1/2   cup chopped onion
1   teaspoon poultry seasoning or sage

Mix corn bread with crumbs and add stock. Beat eggs slightly, add milk, salt, and pepper. Add to the bread mixture. Then add chopped celery, poultry seasoning, and chopped onion and bake in a well-greased pan at 375 degrees F. 30 to 40 minutes or use for the stuffing inside a hen or turkey.

Serves 8

Hush Puppy

Salt and pepper and meal the fish that has been cut up.
Fry in deep fat. Then fry the hush puppies in this fat.

2   cups stone ground yellow corn meal
1   tablespoon unbleached flour
1   teaspoon baking powder
1   teaspoon baking soda
1   teaspoon sea salt
6   tablespoons finely chopped onion
1   fertile egg, beaten
1   cup buttermilk

Mix and sift all dry ingredients. Add the chopped onion.
Combine the beaten egg with the milk. Add to dry ingredients. Drop by spoonfuls into deep, hot, cold-pressed cooking oil or into the hot grease left from frying the fish a few
moments before. When done, hush puppies will float. Drain
on brown paper or paper towels. Serve immediately.

Makes 18–20

Boiled Grits

3   cups water
1½   cups white hominy grits
1/4   teaspoon sea salt
1/2   cup milk
1   tablespoon butter or soy margarine

In a heavy 2 quart saucepan bring the water and salt to a
boil over high heat. Pour in the grits slowly. Stir constantly
with a wooden spoon to keep the mixture smooth. Lower
heat and simmer tightly covered for 30 minutes. If grits become too thick while cooking, add a small amount of boiling water and stir rapidly. Stir in the butter or margarine.
Serve in mounds. Place a poached egg on top of the mound
for a good breakfast.

Serves 4

Fried Grits

2   cups cooked grits from the BOILED GRITS recipe
     (p. 20)
2   fertile eggs, lightly beaten
2   tablespoons water
1   cup finely ground corn meal
1/2   cup unbleached flour
1/2   teaspoon sea salt
cold-pressed oil and butter or soy margarine

Pour the hot cooked grits into a shallow pan. Refrigerate overnight. When ready to cook, cut chilled grits into squares about 2" large. Beat the eggs and water together Combine flour, corn meal, and salt. Spread out on waxed paper. Fill a heavy iron skillet with half vegetable oil and half margarine. Place over moderate heat. Dip the squares of grits in the beaten egg mixture and then place them in the corn meal mixture, turning until completely coated. Fry them in the hot oil mixture until lightly browned and crisp on both sides. Serve with syrup and any breakfast meat. These would be good served as a light supper.

Serves 4

Grits and Cheese Biscuits

These biscuits are good served with a soup and salad or with ham and egg supper. They are just as good warmed up for the next meal if there are any leftovers. Also they would make a different appetizer cut into smaller pieces or small circles. You could add a little chopped ham to the dough before rolling if you like.

1½   cups unbleached sifted flour
4   teaspoons baking powder
1   teaspoon sea salt
1/2   cup hominy grits, uncooked
1/2   cup butter or soy margarine
1   cup grated sharp natural cheddar cheese
1/2   cup milk
1/4   cup finely chopped onion
1/4   cup finely chopped cooked ham (optional)

22

Sift the flour, baking powder, and salt together. Stir in the grits. Cut in the butter or margarine until the mixture resembles coarse meal. Stir in the onion and the cheese and the ham, if desired. Gradually add milk, stirring lightly until just dampened. Shape dough into a ball and turn out onto a lightly-floured board. Knead gently a few times. Sprinkle board with 1 tablespoon grits. Roll the dough out on the board to form a 9" × 10" rectangle. Using a sharp knife, cut dough into eight 1" wide stripes and cut each strip into three pieces. Place about 1" apart on an ungreased cookie sheet. Bake at 425 degrees F. for 10–12 minutes or until lightly browned. Serve hot.

Serves 6

Beaten Biscuits

The beaten biscuit is a dainty biscuit traditionally served with Virginia ham. The object of the beating is to distribute air well through the mass, which expanding by the heat of baking, makes the biscuits light.

4   cups unbleached white flour
1/2   teaspoon sea salt, mixed in with the flour
1   heaping tablespoon butter or shortening
equal parts cold milk and water to make a very stiff dough

Cut the butter or shortening into the flour and salt. Add enough liquid to make a very stiff dough that will still stick together. Empty dough onto a floured board or marble slab and beat with a mallet or rolling pin "steadily half hour by the clock" as one old recipe directs. Fold over and start afresh as the dough beats thin, dredging in flour if it begins to stick. The dough should be firm, elastic, and beginning to "blister" as it nears being ready to roll. Roll a little if necessary to about 1/2" thickness. Cut with a small biscuit cutter. Prick lightly all over the top of each biscuit with a fork. Arrange on a baking sheet, biscuits not touching. Bake in 450 degrees F. oven until delicately browned.

Serves 6–8

Ganny's Biscuits

Nothing smelled or tasted better to me during visits to my grandmother's house than her breakfast biscuits. Early in the morning the smell of them cooking was an invitation to get up and get out of bed. Upon entering the warm kitchen who could resist her offer of "Take two and butter 'em while they're hot."

2   cups sifted unbleached flour
2½   teaspoons baking powder
3/4 teaspoon sea salt
4   tablespoons butter or soy margarine or cold-pressed oil
     (she uses white shortening)
2/3 cup milk (add a little more if it needs it to make a
     workable dough)

Sift the flour with the baking powder and salt into a bowl. Cut in the butter, margarine, or oil that you choose to use into the dry mixture with a fork until it is like coarse meal. Add the milk, mixing until a soft dough is formed. Turn the dough out onto a lightly floured board and knead about half a minute. You should handle this as little as possible. Pat the dough to about 1/2" thick or roll lightly if you prefer. Cut with a biscuit cutter. Place on an ungreased baking sheet. Bake in a preheated oven at 450 degrees F. about 12 minutes or until lightly golden. Serve hot with butter. Use 1 cup whole wheat flour and 1 cup unbleached flour for WHOLE WHEAT BISCUITS.

Makes 10 2" biscuits

Ganny's Buttermilk Biscuits

For buttermilk biscuits use the previous recipe, but add 1/4 teaspoon baking soda and use 2/3 to 3/4 cup buttermilk instead of the sweet milk.

Whole Wheat Biscuits

The whole wheat and the potato biscuits use the same general method of preparation. The whole wheat flour makes the old standby into a heartier biscuit.

1/2   cup whole wheat flour
1   cup sifted unbleached flour
1/4   teaspoon baking powder
1/2   teaspoon sea salt
4   tablespoons butter or soy margarine
1/2   to 2/3 cup buttermilk

Put unsifted whole wheat flour in a mixing bowl. Sift other dry ingredients and add the whole wheat flour. Cut in butter or margarine. Add milk to form a soft dough. Toss on a lightly floured board and knead just enough to make the mixture smooth. Roll to 1/2" thickness and cut with 2" cutter. Place in a pan or on a cookie sheet and bake in a preheated 450 degrees F. oven for 12–15 minutes.

Makes 10–12 biscuits

Potato Biscuits

This light variation of the basic biscuit uses one of the favorite Southern vegetables, the sweet potato.

2   cups sifted unbleached flour
3   teaspoons baking powder
1   teaspoon sea salt
2   tablespoons pulverized raw sugar
1/4   cup melted butter or soy margarine
3/4   cup mashed cooked sweet potatoes (this could be leftover baked sweet potatoes)
1/2   teaspoon baking soda
3/4   cup buttermilk

25

Preheat the oven to 400 degrees F. Sift the flour with the baking powder and salt. Combine sugar, butter and mashed potatoes, beating with a fork until light and fluffy. Stir baking soda into buttermilk; pour into dry ingredients. Add potato mixture, stirring only until moistened. Turn out dough on lightly floured board. Knead about 10 times to form a soft dough. Gently roll dough to about 3/4" thick. Cut straight down into dough with a floured 2" biscuit cutter. Place on an ungreased cookie sheet. Bake at 400 degrees F. for 20 minutes or until golden brown. Serve hot.

Makes 10 biscuits

Cheese Biscuits

1/2 lb. grated natural cheddar cheese
1/2 lb. butter or soy margarine, softened slightly
2 cups unbleached white flour
1/4 cup *very* finely chopped pecans
1 fertile egg, well beaten

Cream the butter and cheese together and add the flour. Beat all together in a cool place. Roll out on a lightly floured board to about 1/2" thick. Cut into any desired shape. Brush the tops with beaten egg and place on an ungreased cookie sheet. Sprinkle tops with nuts. Bake in a 350 degrees F. oven until golden brown. Sprinkle with sea salt and let stand a few minutes before removing.

Makes 4 dozen little biscuits

Foolproof Dumplings

You can't miss with this easy dumpling recipe. Dumplings are used a lot in Southern cooking. They are dropped into soups, broths and stews such as chicken stew.

2   cups sifted unbleached white flour (or half whole wheat flour)
1   tablespoon baking powder
1   teaspoon sea salt
1   cup milk
2   tablespoons soy powder
2   teaspoons toasted wheat germ (optional)
soup, broth, or stew

Stir soy powder, wheat germ, flour, baking powder, and salt together. Add the milk and stir until smooth. Drop by spoonfuls into simmering soup or other liquid. Cover and cook for 15 minutes. Do not uncover during cooking time.

Makes enough dumplings for one pot of soup, broth, or stew.

J.D.'s Easy Rolls

1/4   cup soy margarine or butter or 3 tablespoons cold-pressed oil (white shortening is traditionally used)
1/4   cup raw pulverized sugar
1   teaspoon sea salt
1   fertile egg
1   package yeast dissolved in 1 cup warm water
3   cups unbleached white flour

Cream the butter or shortening with the sugar and salt. Beat in the egg. Stir in the yeast dissolved in the water, mixing all together well. Stir in the flour. Refrigerate the dough. This may be from several hours to 2 or 3 days. Take out and knead. Roll and cut with cutter or with knife into desired shape. Let them stand in pan or on cookie sheet until doubled in size, about 1½ hours. Bake in a 375 degrees F. oven 12–15 minutes.

Makes 18–20 rolls

Good 'n' Easy Pancakes

These are the ones my daddy made when he was in a hurry. The recipe came from the chef of the Palace Cafe in Louisville, Mississippi, years ago.

1   tablespoon butter or soy margarine, melted
1   tablespoon pulverized raw sugar
1   fertile egg
1   cup milk
2   tablespoons baking powder
1/2   teaspoon sea salt
enough unbleached white flour to make a stiff batter (not too stiff, a little runny)

Cream together the butter or margarine, sugar, and egg. Add the milk and mix well. Add the salt and baking powder. Stir in enough flour to make a stiff batter, but runny enough to pour. Cook on a hot griddle. These can be made ahead of time and will keep 2 or 3 days in the refrigerator. Add a little milk if mixture gets too thick.

Serves 2

J.D.'s Sunday Pancakes

These take a little more time to make, but are worth every extra minute. My daddy would make these on Sunday when there was more time to prepare and enjoy them.

2   fertile eggs
2   cups buttermilk
2¼   cups sifted unbleached flour
2   teaspoons baking soda
2   teaspoons baking powder
1   teaspoon sea salt
2   teaspoons pulverized raw sugar or 2 teaspoons natural honey added in with the milk
4   tablespoons melted butter or soy margarine

28

Beat the eggs until light at a high electric mixer speed. Beat in the buttermilk. Sift together the flour, soda, baking powder, salt, and sugar. Beat into the egg and milk mixture at low speed. Add the butter or margarine. Beat the mixture until smooth at a medium speed. Bake on a hot griddle. Cook on one side. When puffed and full of bubbles, turn and cook the other side.

If sweet milk is used, omit the soda and increase the baking powder to 3 teaspoons. An extra egg added to the pancakes made with sweet milk gives a richer flavor.

Special note: If the eggs are separated, the lightly beaten yolks blended with the milk and the stiffly beaten whites folded into the batter the last thing, the pancakes are fluffier. Sweet milk pancakes are more tender than those made with buttermilk.

Serves 4

Sour Cream Pancakes

2   fertile eggs, separated
2   tablespoons pulverized raw sugar or 2 teaspoons natural
     honey
1/2 teaspoon baking soda
1   cup unbleached white flour
1   cup sour cream
1/2 teaspoon sea salt

Mix the well-beaten egg yolks, sugar, salt, baking soda and sour cream. Add the flour and stir until smooth. Fold in the egg whites which have been stiffly beaten. Drop onto a hot ungreased griddle. Turn only once. If the batter seems a little bit too thick, add a little buttermilk.

Serves 6

Corn Pancakes

These make a delightful change from regular pan-cakes.

2   cups stone ground corn meal
boiling water
2   fertile eggs, separated
1/2   teaspoon sea salt
sweet milk

Add enough boiling water to the corn meal to moisten it and to make it wet enough so that lumps of meal do not stick together. Try to keep the mixture smooth and free of lumps. Separate the eggs and beat the yolks. Add the yolks and the salt to the corn meal mixture. Then add enough milk to make a batter that can be poured onto the griddle. Make the batter sort of thin and at this point be sure that all the lumps are out. Beat the egg whites until stiff and then gently fold them into the mixture. Cook on a lightly greased griddle.

Makes 24 pancakes

Whole Wheat

Cooked whole wheat was used quite a bit in earlier Southern recipes. This 60-year-old recipe is timely to-day with the renewed interest in whole grains.

1   cup whole wheat grains
1½   cups water for soaking
3   cups hot water for cooking
1   teaspoon sea salt

Sort the whole grains and wash thoroughly. "It is much eas-ier to have the wheat cleaned at the mill," the original sug-gests. Soak the whole wheat overnight in 1½ cups water. The next morning drain and wash again. Add the soaked wheat to the salted hot water and boil gently for 3½ hours or until it is tender and has no uncooked starchy flavor.

Suggestions for the use of whole wheat:
1. Whole wheat may be substituted for rice or macaroni and served with meats and gravy.
2. Whole wheat may be added to soups as a substitute for rice and macaroni.
3. Whole wheat may be substituted for rice in any good rice pudding recipe.
4. For a breakfast food; serve whole wheat hot with milk or cream. Stewed or fresh fruit may be served with it.

Cracked Wheat Bread

4¾–5¾   cups unbleached flour
3   tablespoons pulverized raw sugar
1   teaspoon sea salt
2   packages yeast
1½   cups water
1/2   cup milk
3   tablespoons soy margarine or butter
1   cup cracked wheat

In a large bowl mix flour, sugar, salt, and undissolved yeast. In a saucepan combine water, milk and butter. Heat until very warm (120–130 degrees F.). Margarine does not have to be melted. Do not heat over 130 degrees F. or it will kill the yeast. Gradually add this mixture to the dry ingredients and beat for 2 minutes at medium speed of the electric beater. Add cracked wheat and beat at high speed for 2 minutes. Stir in additional flour, if needed, to make a soft dough. Turn out onto a lightly floured board. Knead until smooth and elastic (about 10 minutes). Place in a greased bowl, turning to grease the top of the dough. Cover the bowl. Let rise until doubled (about 1 hour). Punch down. Turn onto floured board. Cover. Let rest 10 minutes. Divide in half. Shape each half into a loaf. Place in greased loaf pans. Cover. Let rise again until doubled. Bake in a preheated 400 degrees F. oven about 45 minutes or until done. Loaves are done when they sound hollow when thumped and when they are loose from the sides and no longer stick to the bottom of the pan. Remove from pans when cool.

Makes 2 loaves

Oatmeal Molasses Bread

1½ cups boiling water
1   tablespoon butter or soy margarine
2   teaspoons sea salt
1   cup uncooked oats
1   package yeast
3/4 cup lukewarm water (about 120 degrees F.) to dissolve yeast
1/4 cup unsulfured molasses
1/4 cup pulverized raw sugar
5   cups (about) unbleached flour

Combine boiling water, butter and salt. Stir in the oats. Cool to lukewarm and stir in the yeast. Add molasses, sugar and 1 cup of the flour. Stir until smooth. Add oats and enough flour to make a stiff dough. Knead 10 minutes or until smooth. Place dough into a warm greased bowl. Let rise until doubled. Turn out onto a board. Divide into 2 parts. Shape each part into a loaf and place into greased loaf pans. Let rise again until doubled. Bake at 400 degrees F. for 40–45 minutes.

Makes 2 loaves

Whole Wheat Strawberry Short Cake

2 cups whole wheat flour
4 teaspoons baking powder
1/2 teaspoon sea salt
2 teaspoons pulverized raw sugar
3/4 cup milk
1/4 cup butter
1 pint strawberries
1 pint heavy cream

Mix dry ingredients, sifting twice. Work in the butter with tips of fingers or fork and add milk gradually. Toss on floured board. Divide into two parts. Pat, roll out, and bake 12 minutes in a 425 degrees F. oven in buttered layer cake pans. Split each cake and spread with butter if desired. Sweeten strawberries to taste, crushing slightly. Put between layers and on top of layers. Top with whipped cream.

Serves 4

Sally Lunn

Although developed by an 18th century homemaker in Bath, England, Sally Lunn has long been a breakfast favorite of Creoles. They bake it like a cake and toast leftovers the second day.

1 package dry yeast
1/4 cup warm water (110–120 degrees F.)
1 cup milk, scalded
2 tablespoons butter or soy margarine
2 tablespoons pulverized sugar
1/2 teaspoon sea salt
3¾ cups sifted unbleached white flour
4 fertile eggs, well beaten

Dissolve the yeast in the warm water and let stand 10 minutes. Meanwhile put the butter, sugar, and salt into a large

33

bowl. Pour the scalded milk over the ingredients in the bowl. When lukewarm stir the mixture and blend in, beating until smooth, 1/2 cup sifted flour. Stir in the yeast and mix well, beating with a large spoon. Add another 1½ cups sifted flour, adding in thirds and beating well after each addition. Add the eggs which have been well beaten. Beat in more flour, about 1¾ cups, enough to form a soft dough. Beat thoroughly at least 5 minutes. Turn into a greased deep bowl large enough to allow the dough to double in size. Brush the top of the dough with melted butter. Cover the bowl with a towel. Put in a warm place, about 80 degrees F. until dough is doubled, about 1½–2 hours. Lightly grease the bottoms of two 9" round cake pans. Punch dough down and beat again for about 5 minutes. Halve the dough and put each half into a greased pan. Cover with a towel and again place in a warm place until dough has doubled, about 1½–2 hours. Bake at 350 degrees F. 40–50 minutes or until the cakes are golden brown. Serve hot and spread generously with butter.

Makes 2 cakes
Each serves 6

Whole Wheat Muffins

1 cup whole wheat flour
1 cup unbleached white flour
1 cup buttermilk
1/3 cup unsulfured molasses
3/4 teaspoon baking soda
1 teaspoon sea salt
2 tablespoons melted butter

Sift together the dry ingredients. Add the milk and the molasses and combine with the dry ingredients, beating until smooth. Then pour in the melted butter. Pour into greased muffin tins and bake in a 425 degrees F. oven 25 minutes.

Makes 12 muffins

VEGETABLES

Vegetables add flavor, character, and valuable vitamins and minerals to the daily diet. If properly prepared, fresh vegetables are a plus for any meal. As meat prices soar, vegetables are one of the most economical foods you can purchase.

Of course, fresh vegetables from your garden or a local farm are best. My health food store sells some delicious organic vegetables year-round. They are always available frozen or canned also. When these recipes call for vegetables, "organic" will not be written each time. It will be assumed that organic vegetables will be used when they are available. If you are not sure that the vegetables are organic, wash them carefully to remove any pesticide residues. Some argue that organic vegetables taste no different from other vegetables. I say that they are wrong!

35

Selecting fresh vegetables is only half of the job. The other half is preparing them so that they retain their color, flavor, and nutritional values. Southerners have the tendency to overcook their vegetables as they boil, boil, boil, the tender young things into a limp mess. The following are some tips for successful vegetable cookery:

1. Never overcook. Bring the vegetables to a boil quickly and lower the heat so that the vegetables will continue to cook just below the boiling point. Cook only until tender.
2. Use as little water as possible because minerals and some vitamins dissolve in the water. Do not pour off the vitamins. Drain and save the cooking liquid for soups and stews.
3. Peel or cut fresh vegetables just before cooking to preserve nutrients.
4. A minimum of fancy flavorings are used in the Southern cooking of vegetables. The three main additions are butter or salt pork, salt and pepper. Seasonings should not be overwhelming. Vegetables are plentiful and easily obtained for cooking in the South, often on the same day they are picked. Vegetables picked, cooked, and served the very same day have rich enough flavors not to require much other seasoning than salt and pepper.

Most of the time at home we ate our vegetables cooked only with salt, pepper, and butter or salt pork. On occasions when we wanted something a little "fancy" for such vegetables as new potatoes, asparagus, or cabbage we'd make a white sauce (page 68) and pour it over the hot vegetables right before serving. When Mama and I went to that much trouble we thought we had made something special! Everything else we cooked without recipes, but for something like that we needed a recipe.

"Ma-ma Oswalt going to the field to gather vegetables."

Long before we had air conditioning at home, Mama would spend long summer mornings sweating over the hot stove cooking fresh vegetables ordered from the store early that morning or brought back from my grandparents' farm. We ate natural organic foods from their farm back then nearly all the time, but we did not call them natural or organic. To us they were just "the good-tasting vegetables from Ma-ma and Pa-pa's farm."

Boiled Jerusalem Artichokes

Jerusalem artichokes are plants closely related to the American sunflower. The knotty tubers or roots are used for food. They grew wild throughout the South and were much relished by the Indians living there. Cooked, they have the flavor and texture of an Irish potato but are not quite so starchy.

37

6   Jerusalem artichokes
sea salt and pepper to taste
1/4   cup melted butter
minced fresh parsley

Wash the artichokes and peel them. Cook the artichokes in 1 quart of boiling salted water until tender. Drain. Serve with melted butter and garnish with parsley.

Serves 4

Jerusalem Artichokes served as radishes

Eaten raw the Jerusalem artichoke is crisp and succulent.

Wash the Jerusalem artichokes well and scrape if desired. Put them into ice water to make crisp and crunchy. Sprinkle with sea salt and pepper to taste. Eat as you would radishes.

Jerusalem Artichokes served as a salad

Wash the artichokes and scrape if desired. Slice them very thin. Cover with vinegar and marinate for a little while before serving as you do for a cucumber salad.

Allow 1 artichoke per person

Boiled Asparagus

One of the South's oldest vegetables, asparagus is elegant yet simple to serve. It is good hot or cold.

Cut off the woody ends and tie the asparagus into a bunch with cotton string. This holds the spears together and makes it easy to lift the bunch out. Stand the bunch upright in boiling salted water. The water should not cover the tips yet. Cook until the stems are almost tender. Now put the bunch all the way under the water and cook 5 or 10 minutes longer. Lift the bunch out by the string and drain. Season with butter or pour white sauce over the spears arranged on a platter. Serve hot.

Allow 4 spears per serving

Asparagus Casserole

3   tablespoons butter or soy margarine
3   tablespoons whole wheat flour or unbleached white flour
1/2 teaspoon sea salt
1   cup milk
3   tablespoons grated sharp natural cheese
1/2 cup stuffed olives, chopped
1   hard-boiled egg, chopped
2   cups cooked fresh or frozen asparagus

Melt the butter. Add the flour, salt, milk, and cheese to the butter, stirring carefully as the ingredients are added in small amounts to prevent lumping. Cook over low heat, stirring until sauce thickens. In a buttered casserole place a layer of asparagus, layer of egg and olives, cheese sauce, layer of asparagus, layer of egg and olives, and the rest of the cheese sauce. Bake in a 350 degrees F. oven for 30 minutes.

Serves 4

Cold Asparagus Plate

This dish could be the main dish for lunch. At supper it could be served as an appetizer plate accompanied by a meat dish, rolls, and iced tea.

1   bunch cooked asparagus, drained and chilled
4   hard-boiled eggs, chilled and cut into halves or quarters
1   Bermuda onion, sliced
8   radishes
assorted pickles
lettuce

Arrange the lettuce on a plate. Place the asparagus spears in the center and arrange the eggs, onion slices, radishes and pickles around them.

Serves 4

Boiled Cabbage

1   large cabbage
butter or white sauce
boiling salted water

Take off the outer leaves. Wash and cut into quarters. Cook in a large amount of boiling salted water in an uncovered pot. Drain and serve with butter or white sauce. Cook only until tender.

Serves 4

Horseradish Cabbage

This is good fixed one day and served the next.

5 cups shredded cabbage
1 quart boiling water
1 teaspoon sea salt
1/2 teaspoon raw sugar
3 tablespoons cold-pressed oil
1 tablespoon lemon juice
1 tablespoon horseradish

Cook the shredded cabbage in the boiling water 7 minutes. Drain and add the other ingredients. Toss to mix.

Serves 8

Carrot Sticks

Good for snacks or as an addition to a cold appetizer-relish platter.

1 lb. carrots
2 cups cider vinegar
2 cups water
1/4 cup sea salt
1 garlic clove for each of 3 pint jars
1 teaspoon dill seeds for each of 3 pint jars
3 pint jars

Peel the carrots and cut into very thin strips. Soak in water in the refrigerator for at least 4 hours or overnight. Bring to a boil the water, vinegar, and salt. Put 1 clove of garlic in each jar along with 1 teaspoon dill seeds. Place one-third of the carrots in the jar and pour the hot liquid over them. Refrigerate before serving. These will keep for a while in the refrigerator without sealing. You may seal them if you prefer.

Makes 3 pint jars

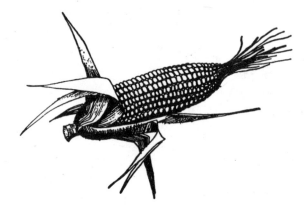

Corn on the Cob

In no section of the country is tender young corn more appreciated than in the South where the housewife serves it in dozens of ways ranging from corn on the cob to corn pudding. Corn on the cob is everybody's favorite.

1   ear of tender corn per serving
boiling salted water
butter or soy margarine

Shuck and silk the corn. Drop it into boiling water. Boil about 10 minutes or until tender. Larger ears may require more time. Drain and serve with lots of melted butter.

Serves 1

Mama's Skillet Corn

This is Mama's favorite easy way of fixing fresh corn.

6   ears fresh corn
2   tablespoons butter or soy margarine
milk or cream (optional)

42

Cut the corn off the cobs. Scrape again after cutting so as not to miss a bit of it. Melt the butter in a skillet. Stir in the corn. Add salt and pepper to taste and a little water. Cook until tender. If the corn is very young and fresh it will not take but about 20 minutes to cook. Tougher corn will take longer. More butter may be added if desired. At the end of the cooking a little milk or cream, about 1/4 cup, may be added.

Serves 4

Succotash

The women of the Southern Indian tribes created a recipe of a mixture of boiled beans and corn sweetened with the fat of the bear. The Indians called it m' sick-quotash, but the English called it simply succotash. This was probably one of the first recipes adopted by the colonists. The Indians had created quite a healthy dish. Beans supply the amino acids lacking in corn. Together they form a complete protein.

2   cups cooked butter beans
2   cups cooked fresh corn, cut from the cobs
2   tablespoons minced onion
1/2   teaspoon sea salt
ground pepper to taste
1   tablespoon butter or bacon fat
1/2   cup light cream

Melt the butter (or bacon fat) in a saucepan and sauté the onion until soft. Stir in the beans, corn, salt and pepper and cream. Simmer until most of the cream has been absorbed.

Serves 6

Southern Corn Pudding

2 cups fresh corn, cut from the ears
2 slightly beaten fertile eggs
2 tablespoons melted butter or soy margarine
2 tablespoons raw sugar or natural unfiltered honey
1 teaspoon sea salt
2 cups scalded milk, heated just to the boiling point

Combine the above ingredients in the given order. Pour into a well-buttered casserole and bake in a preheated 350 degrees F. oven for 45 minutes or until the pudding is set. Spoon out the pudding and serve hot.

Serves 4–6

Lye Hominy

My grandmother Oswalt in Ackerman, Mississippi, until recently made her own homemade hominy by this method. She made it from corn grown on their farm and canned it in jars for the family.

8 cups sweet dried corn
2 oz. concentrated lye
1 gallon water
iron kettle

Mix lye and water in an iron kettle. Bring water to a boil. Drop corn into water and lye solution and boil 30 minutes. Drain and put it into a pot of cold water. Allow water to run over it for about 3 hours to remove all traces of lye. Remove the hulls and black eyes from the corn by hand. Place corn in an enamel kettle. Cover with boiling water and cook until tender. Wash again to be sure all hulls and eyes are off. Season hominy with sea salt.

Allow 1/2 cup hominy per serving (or more)

Hominy made like this may be simply heated and served with butter or used in any recipe calling for hominy. Hominy may be bought canned in most supermarkets if you don't have the homemade which is superior in taste.

Fried Eggplant

The eggplant is native to South America, but has been used as food in the United States since the mid-1800s. It was once believed to be poisonous.

2   large eggplants
finely ground corn meal or unbleached white flour
sea salt and freshly ground pepper
oil, a cold-pressed one such as safflower

Wash and peel eggplants. Slice them about 1/4" thick. Heat the oil. Salt and pepper the slices and dredge them in corn meal or flour. Brown on both sides in the hot oil. Drain and serve hot.

Serves 4–5

Mama's Scalloped Eggplant

2   medium sized eggplants
1/2   cup finely chopped onion
1/4   cup finely chopped sweet green pepper
1   fertile egg
1   cup milk
1   cup crushed cracker crumbs
1/4   cup butter
sea salt and freshly ground black pepper to taste

Peel and slice the eggplants. Cook until tender in boiling salted water. Drain and mash eggplant. Add onion, green pepper, and salt and pepper to taste. Beat egg slightly and combine milk and crumbs with eggplant mixture. Pour mixture into a greased casserole. Dot with butter and bake at 350 degrees F. for 30 to 40 minutes.

Serves 6

Stuffed Eggplant

1   eggplant
1/4   cup chopped onion
3   tablespoons butter or soy margarine
1/2   cup bread crumbs
1½   cups cooked corn
sea salt and freshly ground pepper to taste
dash of hot pepper

Cut eggplant in half lengthwise. Boil about 10 minutes. Scoop out the centers and chop finely. Sauté the onion in butter until soft. Mix with centers, crumbs, corn, salt, and peppers. Stuff the shells. Dot with butter. Bake at 425 degrees F. for 20 minutes.

Serves 2

Boiled Butter Beans

Butter beans are cooked in the same manner as lima beans. The lima bean is larger and more mealy. Butter beans are seasoned with sea salt and pepper, butter or salt pork. Be sure to save the juice for your stock pot.

2 cups fresh butter beans, shelled and washed
4 cups water
1 teaspoon sea salt
1 teaspoon raw sugar (optional)
2 tablespoons butter or a piece of salt pork about 2″ square
freshly ground pepper to taste

Cover the beans with the water in a saucepan. Add the salt, pepper, butter or salt pork, and optional sugar. Boil slowly until the beans are tender, about 1¼ hours. Add a little more water during the cooking if they become too dry.

Serves 4

BOILED SOUTHERN GREENS

The South has an abundance of greens for cooking such as mustard, chard, collards, spinach, beet tops, and the most famous of all, the turnip green. The most common seasoning for greens is salt pork. Bacon may be substituted for salt pork if salt pork is not available. If you do not want to use pork, season the greens with butter or soy margarine.

Save the cooking juice from the greens. The juice is called "pot likker." Actually any juice that is left over from the cooking of any vegetable could be considered pot likker, but most people think of it more often in relation to the greens. Pot likker is eaten from a bowl into which corn bread is either crumbled or dipped. My grandparents, along with most Southerners, prefer their greens, green beans, and all peas cooked to death. My granddaddy swears that they are more flavorable when cooked in a heavy pot for 3 or 4 hours. Ganny says that it doesn't matter that she cooks her vegetables for a long time in a lot of water as long as they eat the pot likker. A light supper could consist of pot likker, corn bread, and buttermilk. Granddaddy would say, "That's mighty fine eating!"

Turnip Greens

The turnips themselves are boiled either whole or diced up with the turnip greens. If the turnips are to be cooked with the greens, cook them awhile by themselves before the greens are added if the greens are going to be cooked only until tender.

1 large bunch turnip greens (turnip greens do not cook down as much as mustard greens)
1/4 lb. salt pork, bacon, or butter for flavoring
sea salt and freshly ground pepper to taste

Pick over the greens. Discard any coarse stems. Wash several times to remove dirt and grit. Place the salt pork in a large pot and add enough water to cover the meat. Cook until tender. If the whole turnips are to be added, do that now and cook about 15 minutes before adding the greens. After adding the greens simmer slowly until tender, about 30 minutes. The liquid will be reduced. Drain the greens and serve with corn bread and a meat dish.

Serves 4

Collard Greens

Mustard greens are cooked the same way. These greens cook down a little more than the turnip greens do.

Remove the crushed leaves and roots from a "mess" (meaning a bunch, sort of, large enough to feed your family) of collards. Wash well. If you want to use salt pork, cook 1/4 lb. in a pot of water until tender before adding the collards. They may also be seasoned with bacon or bacon fat. You could put a little cooked chopped ham in the pot if you like. Cook the collards about 20 minutes or until tender.

Number of servings depends on the size of your bunch.

Ganny's Hot Pepper Sauce

Set a little jar of homemade hot pepper sauce on the table for those who enjoy this poured onto their greens. The pepper sauce recipe is in Ganny's own words.

"Use any kind of hot peppers available and put them into a jar or bottle. I put my vinegar over the peppers in the jar to see how much it will take to cover the peppers. Then I pour the vinegar into a boiler and heat it nearly to the boiling point. Then pour it back over the peppers. I like hot pepper sauce and I like to fish the large peppers out and eat them with peas and greens."

Buttered Spinach

1½ lbs. fresh spinach
½   teaspoon sea salt
1   tablespoon butter
2   sliced cold hard-boiled fertile eggs

Wash carefully the spinach to remove the sand and dirt. Cook only in the water which clings to the leaves after washing. Turn with a fork until all leaves are wilted and tender. Add a little salt while cooking. Serve hot and dot with butter. Garnish with slices of cold hard-boiled eggs.

Serves 4–6

Green String Beans

Several old recipes I have for cooked green beans say to cook them about 4 hours. My mother used to cook them all morning, but has come to prefer them my way, cooked just until they are tender and still hold their shape.

1   lb. green string beans
salt pork, bacon, or butter
sea salt and pepper to taste
boiling water

Wash the beans and remove the "strings" if they have them. Most varieties are now "stringless." Snap the beans into 1" pieces. Cook the salt pork or bacon in boiling water until tender. Add the beans and cook until tender. Cooking time varies according to the degree of doneness that you prefer. Add butter if salt pork or bacon was not used and correct seasoning.

Serves 4

Buttered Carrots

Even my husband who does not like carrots will eat them prepared this way.

1   lb. carrots
butter or soy margarine
chopped fresh dill
boiling salted water

Wash and scrape the carrots. If very small, leave whole. If not, cut in halves or thirds, lengthwise. Cook in a small amount of boiling salted water. Drain. Season with butter or margarine and sprinkle with chopped dill.

Serves 4

Wilted Lettuce Salad

This is another Southern favorite that I enjoyed at my grandmother's. She adds cold sliced hard-boiled eggs to her salad before pouring on the dressing.

4 strips bacon (if you prefer not to use bacon, substitute a hot oil of your choice)
4 scallions, including the tops, washed and sliced
1/3 cup white vinegar
1 tablespoon honey, natural and unfiltered
1/2 teaspoon sea salt
1/8 teaspoon freshly ground pepper
2 heads loose leaf lettuce, washed and drained
2 sliced hard-boiled eggs

Cook the bacon in a heavy skillet until crisp. While the bacon is cooking, tear the lettuce into pieces in a salad bowl and add the scallions and egg slices. Drain the bacon and crumble the pieces over the salad. Add the honey, vinegar, salt, and pepper over the salad and toss gently. The dressing must be hot if it is to wilt the salad. Serve immediately. If you prefer to use the oil, heat it before adding the honey, vinegar, salt, and pepper.

Serves 4–6 depending upon the size of the lettuce heads

Dixie Okra

Okra is the immature seed pod of a type of hibiscus plant, closely related to the cotton plant. A native of Africa, okra is grown in large quantities in the South.

1   cup fresh okra, washed and trimmed
1   medium onion, finely chopped
1/2 sweet green pepper, chopped finely
1/4 cup cold-pressed oil
1   cup tomato juice
1   tablespoon natural unfiltered honey
1   tablespoon whole wheat flour
1/2 teaspoon sea salt
1/4 teaspoon freshly ground pepper

Cook okra in boiling salted water about 10 minutes. Drain. In the oil brown the onion and green pepper. Add the tomato juice, okra, and remaining ingredients. Cook over low heat 10 more minutes.

Serves 4

Southern Stewed Okra

1   lb. okra, washed and sliced into ¼" rounds
1   lb. fresh or canned tomatoes
4   strips cooked bacon (optional)
2   tablespoons bacon drippings or 2 tablespoons butter or soy margarine
1   medium onion, chopped
sea salt and freshly ground pepper to taste

Add onion to the bacon fat or butter in a skillet and cook until tender. Add the sliced okra and cook about 10 minutes, stirring occasionally. Add the bacon (optional) and tomatoes. Season to taste. Cook over low heat until tender, stirring occasionally.

Serves 4–6

Fried Okra

Some people object to the slippery texture of boiled okra. If you feel this way, try fried okra. It's altogether a different taste and texture. Frozen okra may be used if fresh is not available.

1   lb. fresh okra, washed and drained
1/4   teaspoon sea salt
freshly ground pepper to taste
1/2   cup yellow stone ground corn meal
2   tablespoons bacon drippings or cold-pressed vegetable oil

Cut off the stem ends of the okra pods. Cut the okra into 1/4" round slices. Season with salt and pepper. Roll the slices in the corn meal. Sauté the well-coated okra in hot grease or oil until golden brown and crisp. Drain on absorbent paper and serve while hot.

Serves 4

PEANUTS

The peanut, a highly nutritious food, was probably the most versatile and nourishing food that grew wild throughout the South. The Indians used them as a meat substitute by brewing them into thick soups and stews. Also they enjoyed them roasted and salted. The Indians' supply of salt was the sea and they were able to produce crystalline salt by boiling it. The peanut is not actually a nut, but a legume like the soybean and pea. This vine of the pea family has branches which bury themselves in the ground as the plant matures forming peanuts within its pods.

Boiled Green Peanuts

1   lb. young green peanuts in the shells
1/4   cup sea salt
1½   quarts boiling water

Select and wash thoroughly green young peanuts leaving them in the shells. Add the salt to the water and bring to a boil. Add the peanuts and boil for 2 or 3 hours until the peanuts are tender. After 2 hours, open one of them and taste. Serve drained as a snack, letting each person shell his own.

Serves 2

Fresh Roasted Peanuts

1   lb. shelled blanched peanuts
1/8   cup butter or soy margarine
sea salt to taste

Place the peanuts and butter or margarine on a cookie sheet and roast slowly in a 325 degrees F. oven for about 1½ hours, stirring often until the peanuts are brown. Remove, drain and sprinkle with salt to taste.

Makes 1 lb. roasted peanuts

Black-Eyed Peas

1   cup dried black-eyed peas
3   cups cold water
1/2   lb. salt pork or 1/2 stick butter

Wash and sort out the bad peas. Soak overnight. Cover salt pork with a little water and cook 15 minutes. Then put the peas and their soaking water in the pot and continue cooking slowly until peas are tender. Add more water if needed as they cook. Serve with corn bread, onions or hot peppers, and a meat dish.

Serves 4

Mama's Stuffed Peppers

Stuffed peppers are great! Almost anything can be stuffed into a pepper. Start with the basic preparation and the recipe like "Mama's Stuffed Peppers" and vary them from there.

4   medium green sweet peppers
1   medium onion finely chopped
2   whole tomatoes, peeled and mashed
1/4   cup water
2   slices bread cubed
1   fertile egg, slightly beaten
cold-pressed oil for cooking onions (about 1/4 cup)

Preparation of the peppers: Slice off the stem ends. Remove the core and seeds. Rinse. If peppers are large cut in half from end to end. Parboil by tossing the pepper halves into salted boiling water and cooking until almost tender. Drain well.

Sauté the onions in the oil. Add the tomatoes and water. Let cool. Add the bread and the slightly beaten egg. Stuff the peppers with the mixture. Brown in a 400 degrees F. oven until browned.

4 whole peppers serve 4
4 halved peppers serve 8

My Brown Rice Stuffed Peppers

The pecans give the peppers a musky flavor and smell similar to dried mushrooms.

6   parboiled sweet green peppers
1   medium chopped onion
1   cup brown rice
2   tablespoons butter or soy margarine
1   teaspoon chopped fresh parsley
1/4   cup finely chopped pecans
2   cups water
1   cup beef bouillon or vegetable bouillon
1   teaspoon sea salt
1   fertile egg, slightly beaten

Sauté the onion, rice, parsley, and pecans in the butter. Add the salt, water, and 1 cup bouillon. Cover and simmer about 45 minutes until all the liquid is absorbed. Cool slightly and add the beaten egg. Arrange the parboiled peppers on a buttered dish. Stuff the rice mixture into the peppers. Bake in a 450 degrees F. oven until browned.

6 whole peppers serve 6

Shrimp–Brown Rice Stuffed Peppers

Use the BROWN RICE STUFFED PEPPERS recipe, omitting the pecans. Add 1 cup chopped cooked shrimp to the mixture.

Serves 6

Leftover Meat Stuffed Peppers

Use the BROWN RICE STUFFED PEPPERS recipe. Omit the pecans if you wish. Add 1 cup leftover chicken, turkey, or white meated lean fish. Grate cheese over the top and bake in a 450 degrees F. oven for about 20 minutes or until the cheese is melted and lightly browned.

Serves 6

Swiss Cheese Stuffed Peppers

1   cup cooked brown rice
4   tablespoons butter or soy margarine
3   tablespoons grated parmesan cheese
1/2 cup grated natural Swiss cheese
4   tablespoons chopped fresh parsley
sea salt and freshly ground pepper to taste
4   parboiled sweet green peppers

Cut across the stem end of the peppers and remove the seeds. Parboil in salted water until just tender. Combine all the other ingredients and stuff into the peppers. Bake 30 minutes in a 450 degrees F. oven.

Serves 4

Boiled Irish Potatoes

"Irish" potatoes are actually another gift of the American Indians.

8 small or 4 medium sized Irish potatoes
butter or soy margarine
fresh parsley, chopped

Choose fresh firm potatoes. Scrub them thoroughly and leave the skins on. Boil with the skins on because they retain vitamins and flavor. Try eating them skin and all. Actually the skins have more flavor than the potatoes. Boil them until tender in boiling salted water. Serve hot with butter. If you do not want to eat the skins, peel them off and serve them with butter and sprinkle with fresh parsley.

Serves 4

Easy Scalloped Potatoes

This is the easiest recipe I know for scalloped potatoes. There is no making of a white sauce before layering the potatoes. You simply layer the other ingredients with the potatoes and it makes its own sauce as it cooks.

4   medium sized Irish potatoes
    sea salt and pepper to taste
2   tablespoons butter or soy margarine for each layer
2   tablespoons unbleached white flour for each layer
1   cup milk

Slice the raw potatoes thin. Place in a baking dish. After each layer of potatoes sprinkle flour on potatoes, add butter and salt and pepper to taste. Do not sprinkle flour on the top layer. When the dish is full pour in the cup of milk and bake about 1 hour in a 325 degrees F. oven until potatoes are tender.

Serves 4

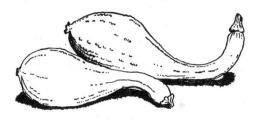

Mama's Skillet Squash

Squash, one of the South's favorite vegetables, was raised along the Atlantic coast before the discovery of America. It is a good source of vitamin A. Use yellow squash in these Southern recipes. If they are not available, substitute white squash or zucchini.

6 medium yellow summer squash, washed and sliced
1 onion, chopped
1 tablespoon butter or soy margarine
   sea salt and freshly ground pepper to taste

Sauté the onion in butter until soft and lightly browned. Add the squash and seasonings. Add just enough water to cover. Cook until soft and tender, about 30 minutes. Squash may be mashed or left in slices. Additional butter may be added to taste.

Serves 4

Every Day Squash Casserole

This was one of our family's favorite squash dishes when we tired of plain skillet squash.

6 medium yellow summer squash
1 small onion, chopped
3 tablespoons butter or soy margarine
1/2 cup milk or cream
1 fertile egg
1/2 cup bread crumbs
   sea salt and freshly ground pepper to taste

Wash squash and cut into pieces. Cook in a small amount of water until tender. Drain and mash a little. Add other ingredients and mix together. Bake in a greased casserole for 30 minutes in a 400 degrees F. oven.

Serves 6

Company Squash

1   lb. yellow summer squash, sliced
1   medium onion, chopped
2   tablespoons butter or soy margarine
3   tablespoons whole wheat or unbleached white flour
1   cup milk
1   cup grated sharp natural cheddar cheese
3   ozs. thinly sliced fresh mushrooms
1/2   cup fresh bread crumbs
1/4   cup finely chopped pecans (optional)
1   tablespoon butter, melted

Cook the squash and onion in boiling salted water until tender. Drain. In a saucepan melt the butter and blend in the flour. Add the milk slowly keeping smooth by carefully stirring every little bit of milk that you add as you go along. Cook and stir until thick and bubbly. Add the cheese and mushrooms. Stir until cheese melts. Arrange half the vegetables in a 1½ qt. casserole. Cover with half the sauce. Repeat layers. Bake covered at 350 degrees F. for 20 minutes. Sprinkle with a mixture of bread crumbs, pecans and melted butter. Bake uncovered 15–20 minutes longer.

Serves 8

Ruth's Squash Rolls

This local prize-winning recipe belongs to Mrs. Ruth Holten, a black woman from Meridian, Mississippi. Meridian's newspaper The Meridian Star *publishes a local cook book each year.*

1¼   lbs. yellow squash, washed and sliced
1/2   cup chopped onion
1½   tablespoons sea salt
1/2   tablespoon pulverized raw sugar
2   fertile eggs, slightly beaten
1   cup cracker crumbs
1   cup corn meal
cold-pressed oil for frying

Cook the squash and onion in a little water until soft. Drain and mash. Add sugar, salt, beaten eggs and cracker crumbs. Chill overnight. Spoon out the mixture into 3" rolls and roll lightly in corn meal. Fry in deep oil.

Makes 10 rolls

Stuffed Yellow Summer Squash

4   yellow squash
2   beaten fertile eggs
1/2   cup grated natural cheddar cheese
1/2   cup finely crumbled cracker crumbs
      sea salt and pepper to taste

Wash squash. Cook whole in a small amount of salted water until tender, but still firm. Drain and cool. Split the squash in half lengthwise. Scoop out the insides leaving enough on the insides of the shells to keep firm when baked. Place the squash in a baking dish with a small amount of water in the dish. Mix together the scooped out squash with the beaten eggs, grated cheese, and cracker crumbs. Season with sea salt and pepper as desired. Fill the halves with the mixture. Bake at 400 degrees F. about 15 minutes.

Serves 8 if squash are large
enough to allow half a squash
per serving

Squash-WHAM Casserole

A new variation of an old favorite in which WHAM, the soy substitute for ham, is used. Of course, if WHAM is not available, ham may be used.

6   medium yellow squash
1/2   onion, finely chopped
1/2   cup diced WHAM or cooked ham
3   tablespoons butter or soy margarine
1/2   cup milk
1   fertile egg
1/2   cup bread crumbs
1/2   cup grated natural sharp cheddar cheese
crushed cracker crumbs to cover the top

Wash squash and cut into pieces. Cook in a small amount of water until tender. Drain thoroughly and mash with a fork. Add other ingredients except the crackers. Mix. Season to taste. Pour into a greased 1 qt. casserole. Sprinkle with the crushed cracker crumbs over the top. Bake for 30 minutes in a preheated 400 degrees F. oven.

Serves 6

Boiled Sweet Potatoes

If a recipe calls for boiled sweet potatoes, drop scrubbed sweet potatoes into enough boiling water to cover. Boil until tender. Drain. Peel and use according to the recipe.

Baked Sweet Potatoes

Southerners eat baked sweet potatoes as a vegetable with almost every meat and to garnish baked 'possums and 'coons.

Wash and dry the potatoes. Rub each potato with a little oil. Bake until tender in a hot 425 degrees F. oven about 1 hour, depending upon the size of the potato. It is done when a fork sticks easily into the centers and it feels soft. Serve on the plate as you would a baked Irish potato with a little salt and lots of butter or soy margarine. Or you may cut the baked potato lengthwise and remove the centers. Mash the centers and season with a little bit of sea salt to taste. Add 1 tablespoon of butter, 1 small beaten fertile egg and 4 tablespoons milk per potato. Refill the shells and bake 20 minutes at 425 degrees F.

Allow 1 medium baked whole potato per
serving or half filled potato per serving

Bess's Candied Sweet Potatoes

Most Southerners love sweet dishes. Cousin Bess's candied sweet potatoes are good with ham, lamb, or chicken.

1/4   cup fresh orange juice
1   cup pulverized raw sugar or natural honey to taste
4   large sweet potatoes (about 3 lbs.), cut up
1   lemon thinly sliced
1   stick of butter or soy margarine, melted

Arrange the sweet potatoes in layers in a baking dish about 15" wide x 2" deep. Pour over the melted butter, sugar, orange juice, and lemon slices. Bake at 350 degrees F. for 1¼ hours, basting a time or two until tender.

Serves 6

Sweet Potatoes and Apples

2   medium sized sweet potatoes, cooked
1   large apple
3/8   cup brown sugar
3/8   cup pecans, chopped
2½   tablespoons butter or soy margarine
1/4   cup buttered bread crumbs

Arrange alternate layers of sliced apples and sliced potatoes in a greased baking dish. Sprinkle each layer with sugar and nuts. Dot each layer with butter. Cover and bake in a 375 degrees F. oven for about 45 minutes or until apples are soft. Remove the cover. Sprinkle with bread crumbs and bake until crumbs are brown.

Serves 4

Sweet Potato Cakes

2   cups cold mashed sweet potatoes
bread crumbs
1/4   cup finely chopped pecans
oil or butter for cooking the cakes

Shape cold mashed sweet potatoes into small patties. Roll in bread crumbs and brown on both sides in a little oil or butter. To add variety, add a few raisins or the chopped pecans to the mashed potatoes.

Serves 4–6

Fried Green Tomatoes

This is another recipe that is supposed to have originated with the Southern Indians.

4   large green unripened tomatoes
1   cup stone ground corn meal or unbleached flour
butter or soy margarine for cooking the slices

Cut the tomatoes in slices about 1/4" thick. Salt and pepper to taste. Dredge the slices in flour or meal. Brown the slices on both sides in a hot buttered frying pan. Drop bits of butter between the slices and cook slowly until they are tender and crisply browned. Serve hot.

Serves 4–6

Mushroom Stuffed Tomatoes

4 tomatoes
1 cup finely chopped onion
1 cup chopped mushrooms
1/2 cup cooked brown rice
sea salt and freshly ground pepper

Wash the tomatoes. Cut across the stem end. Scoop out the centers. Mix together the onion, mushrooms, and rice. Add pepper and additional salt if needed. Stuff the tomatoes and bake in a baking dish at 350 degrees F. for 20 minutes.

Serves 4

Shrimp Stuffed Tomatoes

Follow recipe for MUSHROOM STUFFED TOMATOES and substitute 1 cup boiled shelled shrimp for the mushrooms.

Serves 4

WHAM Stuffed Tomatoes

4 tomatoes
12 pieces of fried bacon or 2 slices WHAM
1 cup chopped onion
1/2 cup cooked brown rice

Wash the tomatoes. Cut across the stem end. Scoop out the centers. Cut the WHAM into small pieces and mix it or the bacon pieces with the other ingredients. Stuff the tomatoes. Bake 20 minutes in a 350 degrees F. oven.

Serves 4

Homemade Tomato Catsup

1   gallon chopped tomatoes
1   cup chopped sweet red peppers
2   tablespoons sea salt
1   pint cider vinegar
1   tablespoon whole cloves
1   tablespoon whole black peppercorns
2   medium sized onions
2   teaspoons paprika
1   tablespoon powdered mustard
1/2   tablespoon whole allspice
1   tablespoon whole cinnamon

Put on the tomatoes, onions and sweet peppers to cook in a saucepan. Cook thoroughly. Put through a sieve and add the ground spices in a cheesecloth spice bag and cook until only half of the original volume. Cook 1/2 hour the whole spices in the vinegar. Then combine with the tomato pulp after the spices have been removed. Cook rapidly. When thick enough, pour into hot bottles and process 30 minutes at simmering. Seal and store.

Makes about 2 quarts

White Sauce

2   tablespoons butter or soy margarine
1/2   teaspoon sea salt
2   tablespoons unbleached white flour
1   cup milk

68

Melt butter in a saucepan. Add flour and salt and mix well, making a smooth mixture. Add milk slowly to the mixture, stirring constantly. Cook until thick, stirring to prevent lumping.

Makes 1 cup sauce

MAIN DISHES

In the South the noon meal is "dinner" and the evening meal is "supper" except for the most formal occasion when supper may be called dinner. Meat is the center of the menu at each meal. The meats vary from chicken to the seafood dishes from the Gulf Coast. Usually dinner is the lighter meal except on Sunday when the noon meal is the heavier one. A company dinner or supper would provide a choice of at least two meats, served with a relish plate, several vegetables, two salads, homemade rolls, iced tea and a choice of pie or cake.

The Southern settlers found a wide variety of wild animals, game, and fish in the streams and lakes. The Indians before them hunted with bows and arrows, disguising themselves in wolf skins as they stalked their prey. There were wild turkeys, quail, squirrels, crocodiles, deer, wild boar, rabbit, and 'possum. Yes, they really do eat 'possum in the South! If you're interested, this native dish is included in the Holiday chapter.

Southerners are very fond of hunting game and it is a favorite sport. My granddaddy Hughes who is well into his eighties and still works full time at his barber shop in Louisville, Mississippi, manages to find a few days off from the shop to go quail and squirrel hunting each fall. A mess of birds would mean an invitation to their house for a feast. My Ganny all these years has without complaint cleaned and dressed what he brought home. As children we relished the taste of the tiny bird brains which we picked so carefully out of the skinned and crisply fried little heads.

Calf's Ears

Never to waste anything, Southern cooks have always cooked nearly all the innards of animals. But look, even a recipe for calf's ears!

4 calves' ears, scrubbed and cleaned well
pot of stock or water seasoned with:
      1 chopped onion
      sea salt and pepper to taste
      2 bay leaves
2 tablespoons butter, melted
2 tablespoons unbleached white flour
1 cup milk or stock
sea salt and pepper to taste
nutmeg to taste
yolks of 2 fertile eggs, beaten
1 teaspoon fresh lemon juice
toast
2 sliced hard-boiled eggs

Scald the ears in boiling water. Remove and rub with a coarse cloth. Then cook in a pot of stock or water seasoned with the onion, salt and pepper and bay leaves for 3 hours. When the ears are tender, take out. Slit the tops of the ears. Simmer them in a sauce made from mixing the melted butter and flour, stirring in the milk or stock, and seasoning with salt, pepper, and nutmeg for 1 hour. When ready to serve, stir in the beaten egg yolks and lemon juice. Arrange on a platter of toast. Garnish with sliced hard-boiled eggs. When a more elaborate dish is desired, extend the slit in the ear and garnish with truffles or mushrooms.

Serves 4

Scalloped Liver and Whole Wheat

4 slices bacon (optional) or 2 tablespoons cold-pressed
   cooking oil
1 onion, sliced
sea salt and freshly ground pepper to taste
unbleached white flour
2 cups cooked whole wheat
tabasco sauce
1/2 cup hot water
1/2 lb. tender calf's liver, sliced

Fry the bacon until crisp. Remove it and brown the onion
in the fat. Push the onions to one side of the skillet. Salt
and pepper the liver and dredge lightly in flour. Fry the liver slowly in the bacon fat or oil until the red color disap-
pears, turning it frequently and adding additional oil if
needed. Cut up the liver and the bacon. Mix with the onion, adding more salt if required. Add a few drops of tabasco sauce. Make a layer of the wheat in a greased baking
dish. Add the liver mixture and continue to alternate the
layers until all the ingredients are used. Pour the water
around the sides of the dish. Cover and bake in a 350 degrees F. oven for 30–40 minutes. Serve from the dish.

Serves 6

Roast Leg of Lamb

*A succulent roast of lamb, a meal to make any day
special or delectable enough for a party.*

1 lamb leg, about 5 lbs.
3 cloves garlic, mashed
2 teaspoons sea salt
1 teaspoon oregano
1 teaspoon paprika
freshly ground pepper to taste
1/4 cup wine vinegar
1/4 cup oil

72

Place lamb in a roasting pan. Mix all other ingredients and rub into the meat. Cover loosely with foil. Let stand in the refrigerator overnight or as long as possible before roasting. Roast, uncovered, at 325 degrees F. about 2 hours to a meat thermometer temperature of 175 degrees. For a leg of lamb allow 25 minutes per pound. Do not overcook lamb. Let stand 15 minutes to set the juices before carving. Left-over cold lamb sliced thin makes good sandwiches.

Serves 6–8

Lamb and Mint Sauce

The South is famous for its mint that grows so freely. This simple sauce gives a unique flavor to the spring lamb.

Leg of spring lamb, 4 to 5 lbs.
1/4   cup fresh mint leaves (or dehydrated if fresh are not available)
1/2   cup cider vinegar
1/2   cup pulverized raw sugar or natural honey
sea salt and pepper to taste

Rub the lamb with salt and freshly ground pepper. Place in a roasting pan. Rinse the mint in cold water and chop it very fine. Dissolve the sugar in the vinegar or stir the honey and vinegar together. Add the mint and bring to a boil and simmer 5 minutes. Baste the lamb occasionally with the sauce. The remaining sauce can be served with the lamb. Cook the lamb 25 minutes per pound.

Serves 6

Pot Roast

The pot roast can't be forgotten since for many the mention of it conjures up memories of Sundays at Grandma's. It was not one of our favorites, but in many homes it competes with chicken for the Sunday dinner favorite.

3   lb. roast
unbleached white flour for dredging meat
1/4   cup cold-pressed oil or bacon fat
3   cups water
1   tablespoon fresh chopped parsley
1   bay leaf
a few peppercorns
sea salt and freshly ground pepper
2   carrots, sliced
4   Irish potatoes, peeled
8   small onions, leave whole
2   stalks celery, coarsely chopped

Dredge the meat in the flour and brown all the surfaces in the oil or fat. Place the roast in a pot on a rack. Add the water and the seasonings. Cover the pot and simmer until meat is almost tender. Add the vegetables and cook about 30 minutes longer.

Serves 8

Southern Hash with Gravy

1   lb. cooked, cut up cold meat in about 1/2" thick cubes
any leftover meat juices
1   onion, chopped
2   Irish potatoes, cubed
1   tablespoon butter or soy margarine
sea salt and pepper to taste
1   cup water
1   tablespoon unbleached white flour

74

Sauté the onion lightly in the butter. Add the flour and blend well. Slowly add the meat juices if there are any available. Add the other ingredients. If there is as much as 1 cup of juices do not use all 1 cup of the water. Instead add the water during the cooking as needed. If hash needs a little more thickening, add a little more flour. Cook it all about 15 minutes. Serve alone or over noodles or rice.

Serves 6

Corn Bread–Tamale Pie

1 cup chopped onion
1 cup chopped sweet green peppers
1 tablespoon bacon grease or butter or soy margarine
1 lb. ground beef
2 cups fresh peeled tomatoes or canned tomatoes
1½ cups fresh cooked or canned corn
1/2 cup chopped ripe olives
1 clove garlic, minced
1 tablespoon raw sugar
1 teaspoon sea salt
1 teaspoon chili powder
1¼ cups grated natural cheddar cheese
dash freshly ground pepper

Sauté and brown lightly the onions, peppers, and ground beef. Add the other ingredients and simmer 30 minutes. Add 1¼ cups grated natural cheddar cheese and stir. Pour into a greased casserole. Combine the following ingredients in a saucepan and cook until thick:

3/4 cups yellow stone ground corn meal
1/2 teaspoon sea salt
2 cups water

Put the corn meal topping on top of the casserole mixture. Bake in a 375 degrees F. oven for 40 minutes. This will fill 2 medium sized casseroles or 1 very large one.

Serves 8–10

Smothered Quail

Squirrel and doves may also be prepared this way.

6   quail (cleaned and dressed) cut into pieces
1   small onion, chopped
2   cups water
1/4   cup cold-pressed cooking oil
sea salt and freshly ground pepper to taste
unbleached white flour

Salt and pepper the quail and dredge them in flour. Brown the pieces in hot oil. Add the water and chopped onion. Stir and cover tightly. Simmer until quail is tender. Serve with rice, salad, and biscuits.

Serves 4

Meat substitutes are not extremely popular in the South as meat is the mainstay of the diet. They just wouldn't feel as if they had eaten without meat, fish, or poultry. Macaroni and cheese dishes are well-liked and there are a few dishes made from soybeans and lentils that go back to the early 1900s.

There are many varieties of soybeans. Experiment until you find one that you like. Don't give up if the first ones taste bland and uninteresting. This happened to us the first two times we tried soybeans. Now we have found one that has a delicious nutty flavor which is good eaten just boiled as they are without added ingredients in an attempt to flavor them. Serve the soybeans boiled in salted water with corn bread sticks and a large mixed green salad. Cook them according to the directions on the package. If they come without directions as do ours bought from a barrel at the health food store, soak them overnight (after cleaning and sorting first). The next day cook them in the soaking water, adding more as they cook, until tender, about 2–3 hours. They are really quite tasty!

76

Lentil and Rice Cakes

These cakes are an old 1900 recipe which produced an imitation "burger" even back then.

1/2   cup dry lentils
1/2   cup cooked brown rice
boiling salted water
1   small onion, chopped
2   teaspoons chopped fresh parsley
pinch of thyme
sea salt and freshly ground pepper to taste
2   beaten fertile eggs
hot drippings or cold-pressed cooking oil
fine bread crumbs

Wash and sort the lentils. Soak in water overnight. Then simmer in salted water until tender. Cook ½ cup brown rice according to directions on the package and add to the lentils. Add the onion to the mixture together with the parsley, thyme, salt and pepper. Form into cakes, dip into beaten eggs, then in fine bread crumbs. Fry in the hot oil to a golden brown.

Serves 4

Noodles and Cheese

8   ozs. flat whole wheat and egg noodles or your favorite noodle
2   fertile eggs
1½ cups milk
1   teaspoon sea salt
3   cups grated natural cheddar cheese
1/2 cup dry bread crumbs

Cook the noodles in boiling salted water until tender. Drain. Beat the eggs lightly and add the milk and salt. Alternate layers of cooked noodles and grated cheese in a greased 1½ quart casserole. Save 1 cup cheese for the topping. Pour egg mixture over the entire contents of the casserole. Combine the remaining cheese and the bread crumbs and cover the casserole with it. Bake in a 350 degrees F. oven 30 minutes. Serve with lima beans, corn bread, and a salad.

Serves 6

Soybean Loaf

2   cups soybeans
1   cup bread crumbs
1   fertile egg
1   teaspoon fresh parsley, chopped
sea salt and freshly ground pepper to taste
2   strips country bacon (optional)
1/2   cup homemade tomato sauce
1/2   teaspoon pulverized raw sugar (optional)

The night before, wash and sort the soybeans. Soak them in water to cover. To cook add more water to the water they were soaked in. Add salt and pepper to taste. Cook about 2 hours until tender. When they are tender drain and put in the blender to make a pulp. I make this up and refrigerate it for several days for use in burgers, meatballs, and meat loaves. Now mix 2 cups of the mixture with all the other ingredients except the bacon. Shape into a loaf or put into a loaf pan. (Double the recipe for a larger loaf.) Cut the bacon strips into half and lay across the top of the loaf. Bake 30 minutes at 350 degrees F.

Makes 1 small loaf that serves 3–4

Soy Burgers

Make these very thin and fry until crisp.

2   cups soybean pulp
1/2 cup bread crumbs
sea salt and freshly ground pepper to taste
1   small finely chopped onion
1   small fertile egg
cold-pressed cooking oil

Mix all the ingredients together. If too moist to shape into patties, add more bread crumbs. Pat thin. Brown on both sides in the oil. Serve on buns.

Makes 6–8 burgers

Glazed WHAM

These glazes would be good for use with the canned WHAM or for basting the slices when heating them in the oven. Arrange slices attractively on a platter and surround with assorted raw vegetables.

Honey and Orange Juice Glaze

1/4 cup fresh orange juice
1/4 cup natural honey
rind of 1/4 orange finely grated

Mix together the ingredients and brush over the WHAM as it cooks. For use with the slices of WHAM, brush them with the mixture after they have been arranged on a lightly buttered baking dish. Heat according to the directions on the package. One half of the recipe would be plenty for use with one-half of a package of WHAM slices.

1 pkg. WHAM serves 5. Makes 1/2 cup glaze

Raisin Glaze

1/4   cup unsulfured raisins
1/2   cup boiling water
1/4   cup raw sugar or natural honey
1   teaspoon arrowroot
1   teaspoon butter or soy margarine
1/4   teaspoon freshly squeezed lemon juice

Mix the raisins and water in a pan and simmer until raisins are tender. Sift the sugar and arrowroot together or stir the honey into the arrowroot. Add to the raisin mixture and mix well. Cook stirring constantly for 10 minutes. Add the butter or margarine and lemon juice. Pour over WHAM slices or over the canned WHAM as they warm in the oven, according to directions on the package.

Makes 1 cup glaze

WHAM Souffle

2   cups milk
1   tablespoon butter or soy margarine
1   cup cheddar cheese, grated
3   fertile eggs
1/3   cup yellow corn meal
1   teaspoon mustard
sea salt, pepper, and paprika to taste
1   cup WHAM, chopped in the blender (or 1 cup ground cooked ham)

Combine the milk, butter, and corn meal and cook in a double boiler for 5 minutes, stirring constantly. Add the grated cheese and stir until melted. Separate the eggs and beat the yolks. Add the mustard, salt, pepper, and paprika. Then add the hot corn meal mixture and the chopped WHAM (or ground ham). Beat the egg whites until stiff and fold into the WHAM mixture. Pour into a greased 1½ quart casserole or soufflé dish. Bake 40 minutes in a 350 degrees F. oven.

Serves 6

Ham Rolls

This dish served with biscuits and iced tea would make a nice light dinner.

24   very thin slices of cooked ham or WHAM
24   cooked asparagus spears
1/2 lb. natural Swiss cheese, grated
4   tablespoons butter or soy margarine, melted
8   small tomatoes
onion slices
carrot strips
sprigs of fresh parsley

Roll up the asparagus in the ham or WHAM. Place in a large greased baking dish. Put a sprinkling of cheese on top of each roll. Pour butter over rolls. Bake in a preheated 425 degrees F. oven until the cheese melts and browns lightly. Arrange the rolls on an oval serving dish and surround with tomatoes, onion slices, and carrots. Garnish with parsley.

Serves 6

"Ham" can mean several things. To some people a real ham is a specially cured smoked country-style ham. It takes more of an effort than it used to take to find a real ham. As a child we got them from my grandparents in the country who raised, cured, and smoked their own hogs. Curing ham is basically a process of inhibiting the growth of spoilage bacteria by the use of curing agents. In addition to preserving the meat, curing adds special flavors depending upon the ingredients of the cure. Country hams are heavily salted or peppered in long curing after which most are smoked to add flavor and extra protection against spoilage. All of the real country-style hams that are cured for a long period of time, whether smoked or not, require parboiling.

Those country hams with that extra-special flavor, Smithfield hams, in order to be called Smithfield must be cured and smoked within a certain radius of Smithfield, Virginia, gotten from a special lean type of hog which is part razorback, and fed partially from peanuts. An aged Smithfield ham, like a lot of country hams, is moldy and must be scrubbed with a stiff brush before it can be cooked. Smithfield hams are a great delicacy. When well prepared their taste is exceptional.

There are several smokehouses that advertise nationally and sell hams and pork products through the mail. Usually the hams ordered from them have been cured, smoked, and cooked and are ready to slice and serve. We serve them for special parties and there is nothing like their special smoked flavor. Even people who normally don't like ham can't get enough of these really good smoked hams. One source of delicious smoked ham and other pork products is *McArthur's Smokehouse*, Millerton, N.Y. 12546. Mr. John Crawford wrote me that they do use nitrites to insure the meats against the ever-present possibility of botulism. However, the U.S.D.A. which regularly monitors their meats and allows 200 parts nitrite per million in the finished product has never found more than 9 parts per million in their meat. Often, he added, there is absolutely no trace. Their meats are never injected with the cure. Rather they are marinated in the curing liquid for weeks and the penetration of the nitrite is slight. Another smokehouse owner, who requested that his product not be listed as one containing niters because of the uncertainty of an impending Federal ruling on the use of these chemicals in some pork products, said that his smokehouse could convert to straight salt curing within a week if necessary. His product would have a darker color, but the taste would be the same, he said.

The majority of hams found in the supermarket today are pale, light flavored "water added" hams. This means that water has been added to the cure and that they have been cured quickly. Usually the curing is accelerated by injecting the curing mixture into the arteries. This method increases the total weight quite a bit and the consumer pays a lot for water and curing agents. This type of ham is more popular with most homemakers today because it requires

no soaking or preboiling. To get convenience flavor is sacri-
ficed, however. Also this is the only type readily availabe to
the consumer in most areas. The hams are cured quickly by
injection and are profitable for the producer and easy for
the housewife. We do not eat these. When we do eat ham
we pay more and get one of the country-style or soaked
and smoked ones. They may cost more, but we are not pay-
ing for arteries pumped full of nitrites and we do get a lot
of flavor for our money.

Southerners use a lot of ham and pork in their cooking.
Some health food cooks say that as long as these meats
come from animals which have been raised on organic feed
under humane conditions that they have no objections to
their use. Bacon, ham, pork, and sausage from nutritionally
fed hogs are rather high in calories, but are good sources of
protein and contain vitamins and minerals. If, for any reason, you do not wish to use ham or pork, please refer to my
discussion of WHAM, a ham substitute, in the glossary
(page 10).

Baked Smithfield Ham

These hams are traditionally served with a special beaten biscuit for which Virginia is famous.

1   Smithfield ham (about 8 lbs.)
cold water
1   cup brown sugar
1   teaspoon dry mustard
1/4 teaspoon ground cloves
enough cider, pineapple juice, or sherry to make a paste
freshly ground black pepper (optional)

Scrub the ham thoroughly with a stiff brush to remove any mold. Rinse well. Soak the ham in cold water overnight or as long as two days if it is a few years old. Drain and simmer in fresh water in a large pot 30 minutes per pound. Let the ham cool in the water. Remove the skin carefully without tearing the fat beneath. When it is cold sprinkle with the pepper if desired. Preheat the oven to 350 degrees F. Make the glaze by mixing the brown sugar, dry mustard, cloves, and enough cider or other liquid to make a paste that can be spread over the ham. Place the ham in an uncovered pan and spread the glaze over it. Bake about 1 hour until the topping has become a glaze. The fat may be scored before applying the glaze. Slice the ham very thin to serve. Serve with beaten biscuits, candied sweet potatoes, and turnip greens.

Serves 20

Ham and Biscuits

There is a special appeal about ham and biscuits. They are good for a snack, at breakfast, for a picnic, or for a party food kept piping hot in a chafing dish or on an electric tray.

20   biscuits made from scratch
thin slivers of country-cured or regular ham, baked

Make your own biscuits. Split and butter them as soon as they are taken from the oven. Put slivers of ham that has previously been baked between the biscuit halves. Serve while hot. For a picnic they are also good cold.

Serves 5

Baked Country Ham with Cider Sauce

This is especially delightful for buffet luncheons or high teas.

7–9   lb. country ham
large pot
boiling water

Basting mixture:
    hard cider sweetened with brown sugar

Dressing:
1	cup fine bread crumbs or cracker dust
1	teaspoon dry mustard
2	teaspoons brown sugar
1	beaten fertile egg

    hard cider to make a paste
    whole cloves for garnishing

Sauce:
1	tablespoon butter
1	tablespoon unbleached flour
1	cup stock, seasoned to taste
1	cup hard cider

Scrape the outside of the ham. Then scrub with a clean stiff brush and rinse well. Place in the pot and cover with cold water and bring to a boil. Skim the water thoroughly. Let it simmer for 2 hours. Remove from the heat and let it cool in the water until just lukewarm. Take out the ham and peel off the skin, which should come off easily. Place in a baking pan and bake in a 350 degrees F. oven, basting frequently at first with cider sweetened with a little brown sugar and afterwards with the drippings from the pan. Allow 20–25 minutes cooking time per lb. When the ham is done prepare a dressing by mixing together the bread crumbs, mustard, brown sugar, egg, and cider to make a paste. Spread the paste over the ham, dot with cloves and bake long enough for it to color a rich brown. To make the sauce, melt the butter in a saucepan and stir in the flour, making a smooth mixture. Slowly add the stock, mixing well to avoid lumping. Cook 10 minutes. Add 1 cup cider. Strain and serve with the sliced ham.

7 lb. ham serves 16

Fried Country Ham and Eggs

A perfect breakfast.

4   slices country ham, cut 1/4″ thick
4   fertile eggs cooked as you prefer

Place the ham slices in a large heavy skillet. Cover with cold water. Bring to a boil and pour off the water. Fry the ham over low heat using the same skillet, without adding extra fat. Cook about 15 minutes or until done, turning frequently. Serve immediately or keep hot while you prepare the eggs. Serve ham and eggs with biscuits or grits.

Serves 4

Broiled Country Ham

One of my grandmother's recipes, this will make a special breakfast or a nice supper.

4   rather thick slices country ham
water for soaking
oil
sea salt and pepper to taste
fried orange or apple fritters (p. 88)

Freshen the ham slices by soaking in ice water overnight or by parboiling in just enough water to cover before broiling. Wipe the slices dry. Place on an oiled broiler pan and brown on both sides. Serve hot with orange or apple fritters and biscuits.

Serves 4

Orange or Apple Fritters

1   apple or orange per person
1   cup sifted unbleached white flour
1   teaspoon baking powder
pinch sea salt
2   beaten fertile eggs
1/4   cup pulverized raw sugar (optional or according to taste)
1/2   cup milk
1/2   cup powdered sugar (optional)
hot ham fat or cold-pressed cooking oil

To make the fritters, slice oranges or apples in thick slices from which all peeling and cores have been removed. Mix together the flour, baking powder, and salt. Beat the eggs and add the raw sugar, if used. Add the milk to the eggs and mix. Gradually add the dry mixture to the wet mixture. Gently dip the fruit slices into the batter and fry in hot ham fat or oil. As soon as they are brown, drain on butcher's paper and dredge lightly in powdered sugar (optional).

Allow 1 apple or orange per person

Stuffed Pork Chops

Pork chops are served often in the South. This is a nice variation on the usual dredged in flour and fried chop.

4   1½" to 2" thick pork chops
sea salt and pepper to taste
4   slices dry bread, cubed and toasted
1/3   cup melted butter
1/4   cup chopped onion
3   tablespoons chopped fresh parsley
1/2   cup unbleached white flour
butter or soy margarine for browning the chops

Cut a pocket in each chop extending from the fat side back to the bone. Salt and pepper to taste. Mix together all the remaining ingredients. Fill the pockets with the stuffing. Tie the stuffing in the chop or fasten with skewers or toothpicks. Flour the chops and brown quickly on both sides in a little butter. Place in a shallow buttered baking pan. Add 1/2 cup hot water and cook at 350 degrees F. for 1 hour, adding a little more water if they cook dry.

Serves 4

Roast Pork

4   lb. pork roast

Put roast, fat side up, in a shallow baking pan on a rack uncovered. Cook at 325 degrees F. until brown and crisp, about 2 hours. Fat will be brown and crisp and all pinkness will be gone from the meat. Pork is usually cooked at 325 degrees F. 25–30 minutes per lb. for a well-done roast (to an internal temperature of 185 degrees F.). Remember that thorough cooking of pork is essential to kill the trichinosis parasites.

Serves 6

Roast Pig

Here is an old Southern recipe for a specialty that isn't served much any more. I have added actual oven temperatures and times that the old recipe did not have.

Get a plump little pig, from three to four weeks old. Wash thoroughly in cold water, inside and out, taking special care to see that the eye sockets, ears, and throat are perfectly clean. Rinse in cold water and wipe dry. Rub over the inside with salt, pepper, and a little sifted sage. Make the dressing and fill the body of the pig with dressing, packing it full. Then draw the skin together and sew with a coarse needle and thread. Roll the ears and legs in oiled paper (today you could use tin foil), bending the fore feet under the body and the hind feet backward. Skewer in place. Put a corn cob or bit of hard wood between the jaws to keep them open. Insert meat thermometer in thigh. Put the pig in a roasting pan on a rack. Rub the skin with olive oil or butter, sprinkle with salt and pepper. Place in a brisk oven (preheated to 450 degrees F.) for 30 minutes. Baste about every 15 minutes with melted butter or oil until drippings have accumulated in the bottom of the pan. Then it can be basted with its own drippings. After the first 15 minutes of roasting, lower the oven temperature to 350 for the remainder of the time. Keep brushing with the drippings and the pig will gradually turn a beautiful brown. When the pig seems tender, which will be in about 2 or 2½ hours, remove the oiled paper (or tin foil) from the legs and ears and cook 15 minutes longer. (Meat thermometer will register 185 degrees F.) Arrange on a large platter a bed of watercress or celery tips. Lift the pig tenderly out of the pan and place on the platter. Remove the stick from its mouth, replacing it with a small rosy apple or a lemon. Put around its neck a necklace of cranberries, popcorn, or parsley. Serve with gravy and tart applesauce. Cole slaw, cranberry jelly, brussels sprouts, sweet potatoes or potato croquettes are all appropriate to serve with roast pig.

Dressing for Roast Pig

1 quart fine bread crumbs
3 tablespoons melted butter
1 large apple, chopped
1 small onion, chopped
a few sprigs minced parsley
salt and pepper to taste
a little milk to moisten the mixture

Mix all the ingredients together. Stuff the pig as directed in the recipe. The stuffing may be varied by using mashed Irish potatoes instead of the bread.

1 12 lb. pig serves 10 people

Quick Southern Fried Chicken

Chicken was once the special Sunday dinner dish. When a family had a fresh spring chicken, they thought that they really had something special. Young chickens were not available all year round as they are now. Serve roast chicken with corn bread dressing, giblet dressing, vegetables, rolls, and tea.

1 3 lb. frying chicken, cut up
sea salt and freshly ground pepper to taste
2 cups unbleached white flour
cold-pressed cooking oil

Sprinkle salt and pepper over the chicken pieces. Dredge in flour. Heat the oil in a cast iron or other heavy frying skillet, having at least 1/2" oil. When the oil is hot, but not smoking, put the thickest pieces in first. Leave enough space for the oil to come up around each piece. Cook at moderate heat and turn when brown. The thickest pieces usually take about 25 minutes to cook. Remove the pieces as they are done and drain on paper towels or brown paper. Serve hot.

Serves 4

Fried Chicken

This makes a deliciously crusted batter for chicken. The added soy powder, wheat germ, and powdered milk give it a nutritional extra.

1   frying chicken, cut up
1   cup buttermilk
2   cups unbleached white flour
3   tablespoons soy powder
2   tablespoons toasted plain wheat germ
1   tablespoon non-instant powdered milk
2   teaspoons sea salt and pepper to taste
cold-pressed cooking oil

In a brown paper bag mix together the flour, soy powder, wheat germ, powdered milk, and salt and pepper to taste. Pat the chicken pieces dry with paper towels or a clean cloth.Then dip each piece into the buttermilk. Then drop 1 piece at a time into the bag and shake until well coated. Continue until all pieces are coated. Heat the oil in a cast iron or other heavy frying skillet, having at least 1/2" oil. When oil is hot, but not smoking, put the thickest pieces in first. Leave enough space for the oil to come up around each piece—don't crowd! Cook at moderate heat and turn when brown. The thickest pieces of a 3 lb. chicken usually require 20 to 25 minutes to cook. Drain the chicken pieces on paper towels or brown paper. Serve immediately.

1   3 lb. chicken serves 4

Roast Chicken

1   5 lb. roasting chicken
sea salt
1   recipe of MAMA'S CHRISTMAS TURKEY DRESS-
      ING (page 179)
melted butter or soy margarine

Rub the cleaned and dressed chicken with salt inside and stuff with dressing (optional). Put chicken in a roasting pan and sprinkle with salt all over. Brush with a little melted butter. Bake in the uncovered pan in a 350 degrees F. oven about 2 hours. When the chicken is done the flesh is slightly shrunken beneath the skin. The thick portions of the breast and thigh are tender and do not run pink when stuck with a fork. The pan drippings will contain along with fat some meat juice that is excellent for making gravy.

Serves 6

J.D.'s Chicken and Spaghetti

This was one of our stand-bys for leftover turkey or baked chicken.

1   baking chicken, about 3½ lbs.
1   cup celery, chopped
2   cups onion, chopped
1/4   cup sweet green pepper, chopped
3   chopped cloves garlic
1   can tomatoes or 3 or 4 fresh ones
3   cans tomato paste
1/2   pound fresh mushrooms, washed, sliced or chopped
1   bay leaf
sea salt and pepper to taste
1   cup chicken broth
1   cup water
2   packages thin spaghetti
1/2   stick butter or soy margarine

Bake the chicken or chop about 3 cups leftover chicken or turkey. Sauté the celery, onion, pepper, and garlic in butter or margarine. Cook until the vegetables are soft, but not browned. Add the other ingredients and simmer 2 or 3 hours. Add more broth or water if needed during cooking. Serve over cooked spaghetti. It is delicious warmed up and served the following day also. Just stir any leftover pasta into the sauce and warm up the whole thing. Serve with salad and bread of your choice.

Serves 8–10

Baked Chicken Hash

This makes a beautiful way to use leftover chicken or turkey and is fine enough to serve guests. A border of puréed peas or mashed potatoes is piped around individual casseroles.

2   cups finely chopped cooked chicken or turkey
1   medium onion, finely chopped
1   peeled raw Irish potato, finely chopped
2   pimientos, diced
2   carrots shredded
1/2   teaspoon sea salt
2   tablespoons chopped parsley
1/2   teaspoon poultry seasoning
1   cup leftover (or canned) chicken gravy, heated
3   tablespoons butter
puréed English peas or mashed potatoes

Sauté the chopped vegetables in the butter about 5 minutes. Mix all ingredients together except the puréed peas or mashed potatoes. Put into 4 individual casseroles or one large 1½ quart casserole. Cover and bake the large casserole 45 minutes in a 350 degrees F. oven. Bake the individual casseroles also covered about 30 minutes. Pipe a border of puréed peas or mashed potatoes around the casseroles. Run under the broiler to brown the top of the hash. *To purée peas:* just put cooked drained seasoned peas into blender and run until smooth, adding a drop or two of cream if needed. Pipe through a pastry bag.

Serves 4

Quick Chicken Pie

The batter will cook up through the meat and make a nice top crust when baked.

1   cup unbleached white flour
1/2   stick butter or soy margarine
1   tablespoon baking powder
3/4   cup milk
2   cups cubed cooked chicken or turkey (if meat is dry, mix 1/4 cup gravy or broth with it before placing on top of batter)

Mix the flour, baking powder and milk into a batter. Place the butter, cut up, in the bottom of a baking dish. Pour in the batter. Do not stir. Place the chicken or turkey on top of the batter. Bake at 325 degrees F. for 45 minutes.

Serves 4

Chicken Pie

Here is another popular use of the chicken. A richer crust could be substituted if you wish.

1   3 lb. chicken, cut up as for frying
sea salt and freshly ground pepper to taste
butter
1   recipe of PLAIN PIE PASTRY (page 146)
1   cup chicken broth

Boil the chicken pieces in salted water until tender. Bones may be removed if you wish before placing the pieces in the pie. Line the bottom of a deep pie dish with crust. Place the chicken pieces in, placing bits of butter between the pieces. Sprinkle with pepper. Pour broth over all. Cover the top with more crust, making slits in the center to allow steam to escape. Bake in a 350 degrees F. oven until crust is done and browned. If you wish, you may double the crust recipe and alternate layers of crust and chicken throughout the pie.

Serves 6

Chicken Salad

An easy way to use leftover chicken or turkey.

2   cups cooked and cut up chicken or turkey
6   fertile eggs, hard-boiled and chopped
2   small delicious apples, pared, cored and chopped
1   cup pecans, chopped
6   sweet pickles, chopped

Mix all ingredients with mayonnaise. Serve on lettuce.

Serves 4–6

Seafood is plentiful and popular along the Gulf Coast States. The recipes of the Mississippi Gulf Coast reflect the Creole influence from neighboring Louisiana. Creole cooking has a provocative quality that is a blend of French, Spanish and Indian cooking given the vivid touch of African cooks. Their secret is in the herbs and seasonings. Creole cooking must be treated as a separate subject, but a few Mississippi and Louisiana recipes with the Creole influence will be included. (see Chapter on SOUPS, STEWS AND GUMBOS). The Southland is dotted with lakes and streams which provide people in most areas with freshwater fish also.

Crab Hors D'oeuvre or Main Dish

Serve in a chafing dish in tiny patty shells as an hors d'oeuvre or in large shells for 8 servings.

1/2 cup butter or margarine
1 bunch scallions, chopped
1/4 cup finely chopped parsley
2 tablespoons unbleached flour
1½ pints light cream
1/2 lb. natural Swiss cheese, grated
4 tablespoons sherry (optional)
sea salt and cayenne pepper to taste
1 pound fresh crab meat

Melt the butter in a heavy skillet and sauté the scallions and parsley until the scallions are soft, but not browned. Blend in the flour. Stir in the cream. Add the cheese and simmer slowly until the cheese is melted. Gently add the crab meat and reheat. Add the sherry and seasonings to taste. Serve in a chafing dish in tiny patty shells as an hors d'oeuvre. For use as a main dish put the crab mixture into 8 large lightly browned patty shells and sprinkle more grated Swiss cheese on top. Run under the broiler just long enough to melt and lightly brown the cheese sprinkled on top. Serve at once with a large salad and homemade rolls.

Serves 16 as hors d'oeuvre
Serves 8 as a main dish

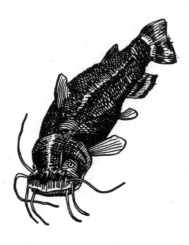

Catfish

Catfish is most popular in the South. It must be skinned after the head is severed. The fish may be filleted or sliced into steaks for frying. It's common to be able to turn down a country road and follow the signs to a "fish camp" built near the water where the fish are caught. The menu would probably be exclusively catfish, hush puppies, and cole slaw.

Catfish, cleaned, skinned and filleted
sea salt and freshly ground pepper
corn meal
cold-pressed cooking oil

Salt and pepper the fish. Roll in corn meal. Fry in deep hot oil. Most people would then fry the hush puppies in the same oil that the fish were fried in.

Allow at least 1/2 lb. fish per serving

Note: To fillet a fish, skin the fish and remove the meat from the side, cutting it as close to the bone as possible. Fillets may be fried, steamed, or broiled. Southerners would fry other fish the same as they do catfish.

Pan Fried Fish

Any fish small enough to be fried whole can be used here, such as perch, stream trout, or carp.

2 or 3 fish per person
corn meal or unbleached flour
sea salt and freshly ground pepper to taste
cold-pressed oil for cooking or butter

Clean and dress the fish. Leave them whole including the heads. Season the fish with salt and pepper to taste. Roll them in corn meal or flour. Fry in butter or oil, turning once. Serve with hush puppies and slaw or salad.

2 or 3 small fish serve 1 person

Broiled Trout

Green and speckled trout from Louisiana waters, relished by Creoles for breakfast, are delicious for any meal.

4   small trout, cleaned and scaled
1/4   cup melted butter
1   tablespoon lemon juice
sea salt and freshly ground pepper to taste
1/2   teaspoon paprika

Set the oven for broiling. Grease the rack. Wipe the trout with a clean, damp cloth. Do not cut off the tails or heads. Arrange on the greased broiler rack. Brush with a mixture of the melted butter and lemon juice. Place rack in broiler with top of trout 2″ from the heat sauce. Broil 5–8 minutes depending on thickness. Sprinkle with a little salt and pepper and 1/4 teaspoon paprika. Turn the trout carefully and brush the second side with the rest of the melted butter mixture. Broil 5–8 minutes longer or until fish flakes easily.

Sprinkle the second side with remaining paprika and salt and pepper to taste. Remove to a warm serving platter. Garnish with parsley. Serve with lemon wedges.

Serves 4

Baked Stuffed Fish

1   fish per person
1/2   cup bread crumbs
2   tablespoons finely chopped onion
1   tablespoon melted butter or soy margarine
1/2   clove garlic, chopped
1   teaspoon finely minced fresh parsley
2   teaspoons dry white wine (optional or to taste)
2   raw oysters
grated natural Swiss cheese
sea salt and freshly ground pepper to taste

Mix together the bread crumbs, onion, butter, garlic, parsley, and wine. Salt and pepper the mixture to taste. Stuff the mixture into the fish which has been cleaned, dressed, and split. Tuck in on top of the stuffing 2 plump raw oysters. Sew the opening together. Put the fish into a greased pan and sprinkle a little Swiss cheese over it. Baste with melted butter as it cooks in a 350 degrees F. oven for about 1 hour depending upon the size of the fish. A small fish may take less time. When the flesh flakes with a fork, the fish is done.

Recipe stuffs 1 large fish

Salmon Croquettes

2   cups canned salmon, bones removed
sea salt and freshly ground pepper to taste
1   onion, chopped
2   raw fertile eggs
4–5   tablespoons unbleached white or whole wheat flour
cold-pressed cooking oil

Mix all ingredients together well. Drop into hot oil with a tablespoon and cook until golden brown. Turn and brown on the other side.

Makes 10 croquettes

Salmon Loaf

2   cups canned salmon, drain liquid and save for sauce
1/2   cup fine bread crumbs
4   fertile egg yolks, beaten lightly
1/2   teaspoon freshly ground pepper
1/2   teaspoon sea salt
4   tablespoons melted butter or soy margarine
1   teaspoon finely chopped parsley
4   stiffly beaten fertile egg whites

Pick the bones out of the salmon. Add the bread crumbs, egg yolks, pepper, salt, butter, and parsley to the salmon. Then fold in the egg whites. Pour the mixture into a buttered baking pan or loaf pan. Bake at 350 degrees F. 30 minutes or until browned. Remove to a platter and pour the following sauce over it.

Serves 6

Sauce for Salmon Loaf

1   tablespoon butter or soy margarine
1   tablespoon unbleached white flour
dash of freshly ground pepper
1/4   teaspoon sea salt
1   cup milk
salmon liquor from can
1   beaten fertile egg

Melt the butter. Stir in the flour, pepper and salt. Cook until frothy. Then stir in the milk and fish liquor. Stir until the sauce boils. Let it simmer 3 or 4 minutes. Remove from the heat and stir in the beaten egg. Pour over the salmon loaf before serving.

Gulf Coast Jambalaya

Most sources state that jambalaya received its name from the French word jambon, *meaning ham. Some Creoles, however, like to tell of a more colorful origin. They tell of the time many years ago when a distinguished guest stopped unexpectedly at a New Orleans inn. The owner of the inn had nothing left from supper to serve the guest. He called to his cook saying "Jean, Balayez" (blend good things together). The guest was pleased with the unusual dish served to him and gave it the name* Jean Balayez *which has since been shortened to* Jambalaya.

1½   lbs. peeled raw shrimp
1   sweet green pepper, chopped
2   cloves garlic, chopped
2   stalks celery, chopped
1   onion, chopped
1/3   cup cold-pressed cooking oil or butter
dash cayenne pepper
dash paprika
1   cup diced cooked ham
2   cups canned or peeled fresh tomatoes
2   cups chicken broth
1   bay leaf
1/4   teaspoon thyme
2   tablespoons fresh parsley, chopped
sea salt and freshly ground pepper to taste
1   cup raw natural brown rice

Sauté slowly in the oil the chopped pepper, onion, garlic, and celery, cooking about 15 minutes. Then add the tomatoes and the salt and peppers, diced ham, bay leaf, thyme, and parsley. Cook 15 minutes longer. Then add the raw shrimp and cook another 15 minutes. Add the raw rice and about 1½ cups water. Cover and let it all cook about 35 minutes more. The rice should be done and the mixture quite dry. Serve with a green salad and hot bread or rolls.

Serves 4

Fried Oysters

2   pints fresh oysters, drained
2   fertile eggs, beaten
sea salt and freshly ground pepper
corn meal or unbleached flour
cold-pressed cooking oil

Salt and pepper the drained oysters. Dip the oysters in the egg and then into the corn meal or flour. Drop in hot oil and fry until they are a light brown.

Serves 4

Deviled Oysters

50   oysters
1   cup fine bread crumbs
3   fertile eggs, well beaten
1   teaspoon freshly ground black pepper or to taste
dash of red pepper
1   onion, chopped
1/2   stick butter or soy margarine
pinch salt

Put oysters in a bowl and chop fine. Put them in a skillet with peppers and salt and simmer while you brown the onions. Lightly brown the onions in the butter. Add the bread crumbs with the well beaten eggs to the oysters. Add the onions and let simmer until some of the liquid cooks out. Put into oyster shells. Cover with some extra bread crumbs. Dot with butter and bake in a 450 degrees F. oven until bread crumbs are browned.

Serves 6

Corn and Oyster Casserole

3   cups cracker crumbs
20   oysters
4   cups cooked corn (or cream style)
1/2   cup cream
1   cup liquid from the oysters
1/2   cup butter or soy margarine, melted
sea salt and freshly ground pepper to taste

Melt the butter in a skillet over low heat. Add the cracker crumbs and toss lightly until slightly brown. Then take a fairly deep casserole so as to have three layers beginning and ending with cracker crumbs with corn and oysters in between. Just put one cup of cracker crumbs in the bottom of the casserole. Alternate layers of crackers, oysters, and corn, seasoning each layer with salt and pepper, and pouring a little butter between each layer. Pour the liquid and cream gently over the top layer of crumbs. Bake in a 375 degrees F. oven for 45–50 minutes.

Serves 6

Baked Oysters

1   quart oysters, drained
2   teaspoons finely chopped fresh parsley
2   tablespoons finely chopped onion
1/4   teaspoon sea salt
1   teaspoon freshly squeezed lemon juice
1¼   cups cracker crumbs
2   cups milk
1   cup light cream
6   tablespoons butter or margarine
cayenne pepper to taste

Butter a shallow casserole. Put a layer of oysters in the bottom. Sprinkle a little parsley, onions, salt and pepper, and a little lemon juice over the oyster layer. Sprinkle a few cracker crumbs. Then add another layer of oysters, parsley, onions, and crumbs. Mix the milk and the cream. Pour milk and cream mixture over the contents of the casserole. Dot with slices of butter. Bake in a 325 degrees F. oven for 30 minutes.

Serves 6

Shrimp Creole

1   cup chopped onion
1   cup chopped sweet green pepper
1   garlic clove, chopped
2   tablespoons melted butter or soy margarine
2   cups canned or fresh tomatoes
1/8   teaspoon paprika
sea salt and freshly ground pepper to taste
1/2   lb. cooked, peeled shrimp
2   cups cooked brown rice

Brown the onion, green pepper, and garlic in butter. Let simmer until pepper is tender. Add tomatoes and seasonings. Boil 5 minutes. Add the shrimp and boil 10 minutes longer. Serve on a bed of hot cooked brown rice.

Serves 4

Boiled Gulf Shrimp

Serve in shells and let each person shell his own for informal serving. It's more fun!

3   lbs. raw shrimp, washed
1   bag of shrimp boil*
sea salt to taste
1   lemon
cocktail sauce

* Shrimp boil is a combination of mixed spices available loose in a box or in a bag.

Bring salted water and shrimp boil to a boil in a large pot. Add the shrimp and boil for about 20 minutes. It may take a few minutes longer if the shrimp are the very large ones. Drain the shrimp as soon as they are done. Shrimp may be served warm or cooled. If you prefer them ice cold, prepare them in advance and refrigerate until ready to serve. Serve with cocktail sauce and lemon slices. A salad and hot bread makes this a nice meal.

Serves 4–5

Cocktail Sauce

2   cups homemade catsup (p. 68)
1/2   cup horseradish
juice of 1 lemon
sea salt and freshly ground pepper to taste
pinch of pulverized raw sugar

Mix all the ingredients and chill 30 minutes before serving. Serve in a little bowl for dipping. This sauce can be used for shrimp or any seafood.

Makes about 2 cups

Shrimp Salad

Nice for a light dinner with relish garnishes and little rolls.

2   cups cooked, peeled shrimp
2   hard-boiled eggs
1   cup chopped celery
sea salt to taste
1   cup mayonnaise
1/2   cup sweet cucumber pickles
1   teaspoon dry mustard
white pepper
2   teaspoons finely minced onions

Chop the pickles and eggs and break the shrimp into two pieces if they are large. Mix all the other ingredients together with the shrimp mixture with a fork. Chill and serve on crisp lettuce.

Serves 4

SOUPS, STEWS, AND GUMBOS

Imagine the aroma of stew or soup cooked all day in a heavy black iron kettle over the open fireplace and ladled out into deep bowls. Soups and stews have long been a wonderful way to use whatever ingredients that you have on hand. Improvise with your soups and stews. Don't be afraid to add something extra if you think that it would be good. Many of the soups and stews in this chapter would need only a salad, bread, and a dessert to make a hearty meal.

Famous Southern soups and stews range from Virginia's famous peanut soup and Brunswick Stew to the gumbos of the Deep South Gulf Coast. Many recipes were based on Indian dishes as in the case of Brunswick Stew which the Indians had made for many years with a base of squirrel meat. The secret of New Orleans gumbo is filé powder introduced by the Choctaw Indians living on the reservation on Bayou Lacombe near Mandeville, Louisiana. They first sold this powder made from dried young sassafras leaves in the Creole markets for medicinal purposes. The early Creole cooks soon discovered that filé powder had a delicate flavor as well as a glutinous quality and began to put it into their soups and stews. Because the Indian word for sassafras was *kombo* the Creoles adopted "gumbo" to describe their soup to which filé powder was added.

Special Dumplings

For good eating, nothing can surpass the good old-fashioned farm style stews with dumplings. Make hearty stews with any kind of meat you have on hand and your own favorite combinations of fresh vegetables. You'll like these dumplings with the special seasonings.

2   cups sifted unbleached white flour
2½   teaspoons baking powder
1   teaspoon sea salt
1   cup milk

Sift flour once. Add baking powder and salt and sift into mixing bowl. Add milk and stir until flour is dampened. Drop from a spoon into simmering stew, resting dumplings on top of meat or vegetables. Cover tightly and cook gently without removing cover 15 minutes or a little more depending upon the size of the dumplings.

Makes 12 medium dumplings

Variations:
PARSLEY DUMPLINGS—Add 1 tablespoon finely chopped fresh parsley to the flour mixture. Good with veal stew or chicken stew.
TOMATO DUMPLINGS—Instead of milk use tomato juice for the liquid. Good with beef stew.
CURRY DUMPLINGS—Sift 1 teaspoon curry powder in with the other dry ingredients. Good with lamb stew or chicken stew.
BASIL DUMPLINGS—Add 2 teaspoons finely chopped fresh basil to the flour mixture. Good with beef stew.

109

File Gumbo

This is based on the recipe said to have belonged to Mrs. Jefferson Davis whose recipe began "Take one old chicken cut into joints and bits."

1   chicken cut into pieces (head and legs omitted)
1   dozen large oysters in their liquor
3   slices unboiled country ham or regular uncooked ham
half an onion, sliced
a bunch of sweet herbs tied into a muslin bundle
1   carrot sliced thin
4   whole cloves
3   pinches mace
a pinch nutmeg
sea salt to taste
pinch cayenne pepper
1   tablespoon filé powder
cold-pressed cooking oil

Fry the chicken to a light golden brown in a little cold-pressed oil. Add the seasoning, ham, and herbs and simmer for several hours. For a 6 o'clock supper, put the gumbo on to cook at 1 o'clock. When the chicken has fallen off the bones and is in shreds take out the bag of herbs and the cloves. Put in the oysters and their liquor just long enough to plump them and to curl their edges. Add the filé just as the pot is taken from the stove. *The filé should not boil.* Serve this in large individual bowls over hot cooked rice.

Serves 6–8

Use filé powder sparingly and do not let it boil. If you do, it will not be fit to eat. Fresh okra may be used instead of filé powder. Use one or the other, but not both.

Mrs. Tingle's Shrimp Gumbo

The Tingles own and run a little neighborhood meat market in Meridian, Mississippi, where you can be sure of getting good fresh meat and seafood brought up from the Gulf.

1 ham hock or 1 lb. cut-up ham or 1 soup bone or 1 lb. cut-up beef
5 or 6 fresh tomatoes
1 cup celery, chopped
1 onion, chopped
1 lb. raw shrimp, peeled
1¼ cups fresh or frozen okra
2 cups fresh corn cut off the cobs
1 teaspoon sugar
2 cups brown rice
sea salt and freshly ground pepper to taste
4 to 6 cups water (part of this may be chicken broth)

Measure 4 to 6 cups water (some chicken broth may be used if you have it) in a large pot. Add the tomatoes, celery, onion, meats, and salt and pepper to taste. Bring to a boil. Reduce heat and simmer for 2½ hours. Add the shrimp and okra and cook 30 minutes longer. Before the last 30 minutes of cooking put the rice on to cook in another saucepan. When the rice is done put some in each bowl and serve the gumbo on top of the rice. You can add crab meat or chicken to the basic mixture if you have it.

Serves 6

Stewed Okra Gumbo

Since cooked okra gives the same slippery smoothness and the same results many okra dishes are also called "gumbos."

1   lb. okra, washed and sliced
2½   cups fresh tomatoes, peeled and chopped
4   strips bacon cut into pieces (optional) or 1 tablespoon cold-pressed oil
1   medium sized onion, chopped
sea salt and freshly ground pepper to taste

Fry the bacon and remove from the grease. Add the onion to the bacon fat and cook until tender, but not brown. Add okra and cook about 10 minutes. Add cooked bacon and tomatoes. Season to taste. Cook over low heat until tender stirring occasionally. Serve in bowls over cooked rice or without rice according to preference.

Serves 4

Barley Soup

2   lbs. stew meat or soup bones
1   cup barley
1   onion, sliced
a bay leaf
1   carrot, sliced thin
1   stalk celery, sliced thin
2   cloves
1   tablespoon butter or soy margarine
1   tablespoon whole wheat flour
sea salt and freshly ground pepper to taste

Cover the beef or bones with cold water and boil. When boiling skim it well and then allow to simmer for 3 hours. An hour before serving, add the barley, onion, bay leaf, carrot, celery, cloves and butter. Mix the flour into a paste with a little cold water and stir into the soup and cook 5 minutes more. Season with salt and pepper to taste.

Serves 8

Brunswick Stew

Southside, Virginia, in the county of Brunswick has the first recorded appearance of Brunswick Stew. It was supposedly based on an Indian concoction of squirrel, vegetables, and seasonings. It is now usually made with chicken.

3/4 lb. chicken parts
1 bay leaf
1 Irish potato, peeled and sliced
1 onion, sliced
1 package frozen mixed vegetables or 2 cups fresh mixed vegetables such as butter beans, corn, and carrots, diced
2 fresh peeled tomatoes
4 tablespoons butter or soy margarine
sea salt and freshly ground pepper to taste
1 tablespoon unbleached flour

Boil chicken gently in lightly salted water with bay leaf until tender. Remove and set aside the chicken. Add potato, onion, vegetables and tomatoes to the chicken broth and boil gently until all are tender. Meanwhile remove bones and skin from the cooked chicken. Cut into bite size pieces and add to the broth. Add butter and seasonings. Bring to a boil. Mix flour and a little cold water to make a smooth paste. Stir the paste into the stew. Simmer until thickened.

Serves 4

Stewed Chicken and Dumplings

*Every Southern cook makes chicken and dumplings,
therefore there are many versions of this old favorite.
This recipe is an easy and very delicious one.*

1   cut up chicken
1   teaspoon chopped onion
4   tablespoons butter or soy margarine, melted
sea salt and freshly ground pepper to taste
2   tablespoons unbleached white flour or 2 teaspoons ar-
    rowroot
FOOLPROOF DUMPLINGS (page 26) or GANNY'S
BISCUITS (page 24)

Put the chicken pieces into a large pot for cooking. Cover
with cold water and cook until almost tender. Add the
chopped onion, salt and pepper. Mix the butter or margarine and flour and add to the stew for thickening. Cook
until the chicken is tender. Meanwhile make a batch of
FOOLPROOF DUMPLINGS. When the chicken is tender
drop them by the spoonful into the stew. Cover and cook 15
minutes without removing the lid. Or you may make a recipe
of GANNY'S BISCUITS (page 24) for the dumpling
dough. Roll the biscuit dough thin and cut dumplings 3"
long and 2" wide and drop them in and cook covered for
15 minutes.

Serves 4

Easy Everyday Beef Stew

This is a good family dish to prepare when you want an easy stew with a minimum of ingredients.

1½   lbs. boneless stew meat, cubed
1/3 cup whole wheat flour
1½   teaspoons sea salt
freshly ground pepper to taste
2½   cups water
2   tablespoons cold-pressed oil
4   medium onions, sliced
3   medium potatoes, cubed
6   carrots, sliced
1½   cups raw green peas or green beans

Mix together the flour, salt and pepper, and beef cubes. Brown the meat thoroughly in hot oil in a heavy pot or Dutch oven. Add any remaining flour mixture to the pot. Add water and simmer for 2 hours or until the meat is tender. Add the potatoes, onions, and carrots and cook covered for 20 minutes. Add the peas or beans and simmer about 45 minutes more or until all the vegetables are tender. Stir occasionally.

Serves 6

Fish Stew

When you want something hearty and quick, this fish stew is perfect. It's nutritious and filling. With a salad and crackers or bread it's a complete meal for dinner or supper.

1   pound fresh or frozen firm fish such as haddock, cut into 1" cubes
1/2   stick butter or soy margarine
1   cup thinly sliced onions
1   cup diced raw potatoes
1   cup water
2   teaspoons sea salt
freshly ground pepper to taste
3   cups milk
1/2   teaspoon crushed rosemary
1/4   teaspoon crushed thyme
1   cup light cream
2   tablespoons whole wheat flour or 2 teaspoons arrowroot
2   diced carrots

Melt the butter and add to it the onion, potato, carrots, water, salt, and pepper. Cover and simmer until carrots are tender. Add the fish, milk, herbs, and simmer until fish flakes easily. Blend the flour into the cream. Add to the stew. Heat thoroughly.

Serves 6

Lamb Stew

1   lb. uncooked lamb, cubed
1/4   cup whole wheat flour
1   teaspoon sea salt
freshly ground pepper to taste
2½   cups water
2   tablespoons cold-pressed oil
4   medium onions, sliced
1   cup green beans
3   or 4 turnips or parsnips, cubed
3   carrots, sliced
1   stalk celery, sliced

Salt and pepper the lamb cubes. Dredge in flour and brown in hot oil. Add any remaining flour to the cooking pot. Add the water and simmer 2 hours or until the meat is tender. Add the other ingredients and cook about 45 minutes or until all the vegetables are tender. Drop CURRY DUMP-LINGS (page 109) on top of stew and cook covered for 15 minutes.

Serves 4

Oyster Stew

1   quart oysters
2   tablespoons butter or soy margarine
2   quarts milk
sea salt and freshly ground pepper to taste

Drain the liquor from the oysters into a large saucepan. Let it boil about 1 minute. Put in the milk and let it just come to the boiling point. Do not boil. Add the oysters and cook without boiling just until they begin to curl around the edges. Take off the stove. Add the butter and salt and pepper to taste. Serve at once.

Serves 6

117

Veal Stew

Make stew as directed for LAMB STEW (page 117) using 1 lb. cubed veal stew meat and fresh vegetables of your choice. Perhaps you would like to substitute lima beans for the green beans. Drop PARSLEY DUMPLINGS (page 109) on top and simmer covered for 15 minutes.

Serves 4

Vegetable Soup

Vegetable soups are just wonderful! Make up your own combinations and once a week make a soup from all the leftovers in the refrigerator. Save all cooking liquids to use as stock in place of all water in soup recipes.

1   large soup bone
1   pound lean beef stew meat
4   tablespoons cold-pressed vegetable oil
1/2   cup chopped onion
1/2   cup chopped celery
1   cup sliced carrots
1/4   cup chopped sweet green pepper
1   cup diced Irish potatoes
1   quart water or broth and stock
1   teaspoon sea salt
1/4   teaspoon freshly ground pepper
1   cup green peas
1   cup corn, cut off the cobs
4   fresh peeled tomatoes
2   tablespoons chopped parsley
1   cup shredded cabbage

Brown the meat in 2 tablespoons oil in a heavy pot. Sauté the onions, celery, carrots, peppers, and potatoes in 2 tablespoons oil in a heavy skillet until lightly browned. Add the water to the meat and simmer 1 hour. Add the sautéed vegetables, salt and pepper, peas, corn, and tomatoes and simmer 1 hour longer. Add the cabbage during the last 15 minutes of cooking time.

Serves 6–8

Croutons

Croutons are squares of stale bread browned in the oven or in a little butter in a pan on top of the stove. Cut the bread into 1″ slices. Then cut the slices into 1/2″ cubes and brown. Serve with cream soups or salads.

Tomato Bisque

This is perhaps the most delicious of cream soups when properly made. If allowed to boil after the milk and tomatoes are mixed, the soup will curdle.

2   cups fresh or canned tomatoes
2   tablespoons butter or soy margarine
2   tablespoons unbleached flour
1   teaspoon raw sugar
1   teaspoon sea salt
1   quart milk
1   teaspoon chopped fresh parsley
1/4   teaspoon white pepper
1   bay leaf

Put the tomatoes on to cook with the spices and simmer 10 minutes. Force through a food mill or strainer. Scald the milk. Make a paste of the flour and a little water and stir into the milk. Add the butter and salt and pepper. Return the strained tomatoes to the heat and add sugar. Allow to come to a boil. Then add the milk and serve at once. Garnish with croutons.

Serves 4

Cream of Pea Soup

1   cup dried split peas
2½   quarts cold water
ham bone
1   small onion, chopped
3   tablespoons butter or soy margarine
2   tablespoons unbleached flour or 2 teaspoons arrowroot
1   teaspoon sea salt
dash freshly ground pepper to taste
2   cups milk

Wash and pick over the peas and soak overnight in the water. Add the ham bone and onion. Simmer 3 or 4 hours or until very soft. Then force through a sieve. Add the butter, flour, salt and pepper to the purée. Add the milk, adding more than 2 cups if necessary. Cook to thicken. Do not boil. Season to taste.

Serves 6–8

Easy Peanut Soup

Virginia is famous for its peanut soup. Some versions are made with peanut butter and their strong flavor is for those who are really crazy about peanut butter. Here is my own peanut soup which is very rich, but mild in flavor.

2   cups water, heated to the boiling point
1   vegetable bouillon cube
2   cups fresh sweet roasted shelled Virginia peanuts
sea salt to taste
chopped fresh chives for garnishing

Put the water and bouillon in the blender. Mix. Add the peanuts and chop to the desired smoothness. I leave my peanuts quite chunky. Heat the soup in a saucepan and serve. Garnish with chopped fresh chives.

Serves 4–6

DESSERTS

The Southern hostess prides herself on her desserts, especially pies and cakes. She feels a need to serve "something sweet" with each meal. An apology is often offered if there is only one dessert served rather than a choice of two or three. Desserts are the test of a good meal and everyone has his favorite.

Cakes have long been associated with the Southern way of living. Some had their roots in Europe and others were original recipes indigenous to the South. Among the favorite cakes are pound cakes, fruit cakes, spice cakes, and various other cakes made with fruits and nuts. There is a group of cakes called the "Famous Name" cakes so called because they bear the name of famous Southerners such as General Robert E. Lee, Jefferson Davis, and George Washington.

Pies, like cakes, had their beginnings from a European idea. Dessert pies were patterned after the English meat pies. Popular Southern pies are pecan, black bottom, chess, egg custard, sweet potato, pumpkin, and fruit pies.

The variety of Southern desserts is endless. Southern cooks love to make desserts and will no doubt continue to devise ingenious ways to use the native fruits and nuts which are so plentiful. Most of the pies and cakes are very rich and filling, but can successfully be prepared with natural ingredients.

Some are desserts for special occasions, not the kind you would prepare every day. For such occasions making a dessert absolutely sugarless would take all the fun out of it according to the Southern way of thinking. Some of these recipes do use raw sugar. The ones that do not call for molasses or honey use pulverized raw sugar. The only difference we can tell in substituting raw sugar for refined is a slightly honey-colored appearance in some candies and icings that would be pure white with the use of refined white sugar. We do not find this color objectionable, but in a few recipes white and raw sugar measurements are both given in case a pure white color is desired.

These desserts are variations of old favorites in some cases. Most, however, were gathered from family members and old handwritten recipes recorded by black cooks in crumbling, brittle composition books. Others came from faded nineteenth century family cookbooks. In these old cookbooks, ingredients were not listed as they are today. There would simply be a paragraph of directions. There were no numbers of servings listed, no baking temperatures or times. Stoves were still wood-burning and the closest temperature might be moderate, slow, or hot. For example here is one such recipe for Plain Baked Custard:

Beat slightly four eggs, whites and yolks, together. Add one quart fresh milk, four tablespoonfuls of sugar, a pinch of salt and whatever flavoring is desired. Nutmeg is the old fashioned flavoring that most people like. Rose water is delicate and almond good, though not so wholesome as other flavors. Bake in stoneware cups or a bowl set in a basin of hot water. Take care that the oven is not too hot.

Fresh Apple Crunch Cake

1½ cups cold-pressed safflower oil
2 cups pulverized raw sugar
2 fertile eggs
3 cups cake flour or 2⅝ cups unbleached white flour
2 teaspoons pure vanilla extract
1 teaspoon baking soda
1 teaspoon cinnamon
1 teaspoon sea salt
3 cups chopped (peeled and cored) fresh apples
1 cup chopped pecans

Mix the oil and sugar together well. Add the eggs and beat until creamy. Add the vanilla. Sift the dry ingredients together and add to the wet mixture. Stir in the chopped apples and pecans. Bake in a greased tube pan 1½ to 2 hours until done. Bake at 275 degrees F. for 1 hour. Then turn oven to 300 degrees F. for the remainder of the time.

Serves 12

Homemade Applesauce

If a recipe calls for unsweetened applesauce, use this one, omitting the sweetening.

Wash the apples that you want to make sauce from and cut into pieces. Cook until soft in a small amount of water. Press through a sieve and add pulverized raw sugar or honey to taste. A few grains of cinnamon, ground nutmeg, or 1 teaspoon lemon juice will give additional flavor.

1 apple makes 1/2 cup

Sugarless Applesauce Cake

This recipe belonged to my great-grandmother Brumfield who noted on her recipe: "We use this cake about once a week."

1/2   cup shortening or margarine (softened)
1   cup unsulfured molasses
1   fertile egg
2¼   cups unbleached white flour
1   teaspoon baking soda
1   teaspoon cinnamon
1/2   teaspoon cloves
1   teaspoon sea salt
1   cup unsweetened applesauce
1   cup unsulfured raisins

Cream the shortening or margarine until smooth. Add the molasses and beat thoroughly. Beat the egg vigorously and cream into the mixture. Sift the flour. Measure it and sift with the other dry ingredients. Add to the creamed mixture with the applesauce, mixing well. Add the raisins last. Pour into a well-greased rectangular cake pan and bake in a 350 degrees F. oven for 45 minutes.

Serves 8

Ganny's Applesauce Cake

2½   cups homemade applesauce, cooled and unsweetened
1   cup soy margarine
2   cups pulverized raw sugar
4   cups flour (2 unbleached white and 2 all-purpose whole wheat)
1   teaspoon sea salt
4   teaspoons baking soda
1   teaspoon cinnamon
1   teaspoon cloves
1   teaspoon allspice
1   lb. natural unsulfured seedless raisins
1   lb. chopped pecans

Take two of the cups of flour and mix into them the soda and spices. Then take the other 2 cups of flour and mix the raisins with 1 cup of the flour and the nuts with the other cup of flour and the rest of the ingredients. Pour into two greased and floured loaf pans. Bake in a 350 degrees F. oven 30 minutes or until a toothpick inserted into the center of the loaves comes out clean.

Makes 2 loaves (which serve about 12,
depending on thickness of slice)

Southern Gingerbread

Southern cooks who could not afford the luxury of sugar substituted molasses and produced gingerbread.

2½   cups unbleached white flour
1   teaspoon sea salt
1½   teaspoons baking soda
2   teaspoons ginger
1   cup unsulfured molasses
1   cup buttermilk
1/4 cup melted butter or soy margarine

Sift the flour and then measure the 2½ cups if flour is not presifted. Sift twice with the baking soda, salt, and ginger. Combine the molasses, buttermilk and butter. Add to the sifted dry ingredients and beat until smooth. Bake in a greased square pan in a 350 degrees F. oven for 35 minutes or until done.

Serves 8

Whole Wheat Gingerbread

1/4 cup butter or soy margarine
1/2 cup pulverized raw sugar
1   fertile egg, well beaten
1/2 cup unsulfured molasses
1/2 cup buttermilk
1¾   cups sifted whole wheat flour
1/2 teaspoon baking powder
1½   teaspoons cinnamon
1   teaspoon ginger
1/4 teaspoon sea salt
1   teaspoon baking soda

Cream the butter and sugar until smooth. Add the beaten egg to the creamed mixture. Mix the molasses and the milk together. Mix the flour with the soda, baking powder, spices, and salt. Add the dry ingredients to the creamed mixture alternately with the molasses and milk mixture, adding the flour first and last. Bake in a greased square pan at 350 degrees F. for 40 minutes. Cool. Cut into squares.

Serves 6

Lady Baltimore Cake

Almost every cookbook has a recipe for Lady Baltimore cake, each a little different. Some cakes are covered on the top and sides as well as between the layers with the nut and fruit frosting. Others call for the tops and sides to be a plain white frosting with the nuts and fruits being only between the layers.

3   cups cake flour or 2⅝ cups unbleached white flour
3   teaspoons baking powder
1/4   teaspoon sea salt
1/2   cup butter or soy margarine, softened
1½   cups pulverized sugar
1/2   cup milk
1/2   cup water
1   teaspoon pure vanilla extract
3   egg whites, beaten until stiff
1/4   teaspoon pure almond extract
Lady Baltimore Frosting

Sift the flour if not presifted. Measure the flour and then add baking powder and salt. Sift together three times. Cream the butter and sugar together. Gradually add the flour alternately with the milk and water, beating after each addition until mixture is smooth. Add the flavorings. Fold in the egg whites. Bake in 2 greased 9" cake pans at 375 degrees F. for 20 minutes. Cool and remove from pans. Frost with Lady Baltimore Frosting.

Serves 8

Lady Baltimore Frosting

2   cups white or pulverized raw sugar
2/3   cup water
2   fertile egg whites, stiffly beaten
6   figs (fresh or honey-dipped dried ones), finely chopped
2/3   cup unsulfured raisins, finely chopped
2/3   cup pecans, finely chopped

Boil the sugar and water to a soft ball stage (240 degrees F. on the candy thermometer). *Slowly* pour the cooked syrup over the stiffly beaten egg whites, beating constantly. Set aside to cool a few minutes. Add the chopped figs, raisins, and nuts to 1/3 of the frosting. Spread this between the layers. Spread the remaining plain frosting on top and around the sides of the cake. Garnish with nuts and candied cherries if desired.

Aunt Lucy's Muffin Cakes

This recipe belonged to Lucy Dunn who was my family's "ironing woman" for many years.

3   eggs
2   sticks butter at room temperature
2   teaspoons baking powder
2   teaspoons pure vanilla extract (or pure lemon extract for a variation)
2   cups pulverized raw sugar
3   cups unbleached white flour
1   cup milk

Cream the butter and add the sugar. Beat until light and creamy. Beat in the eggs. Add the vanilla and milk, mixing thoroughly. Mix in the flour. Pour the mixture into lightly greased muffin tins, filling about 2/3 full. Bake in a 375 degrees F. oven for 15–20 minutes. Delicious hot with butter!

Makes 1 dozen muffins

Buttermilk Pound Cake

There are many versions of pound cakes popular in the South. This easy buttermilk cake is one of our favorites.

3   cups white or pulverized raw sugar
1   cup buttermilk
3   cups unbleached white flour
5   fertile eggs
1   teaspoon pure vanilla extract
1   cup butter or soy margarine
1/3   teaspoon baking soda

Cream the butter and sugar. Beat the eggs and add one at a time to the creamed butter and sugar mixture. Add vanilla. Mix the baking soda in the buttermilk. Add the flour alternately with the buttermilk to the creamed mixture. Bake in a greased and floured tube pan.

Baking schedule:
preheat oven to 250 degrees F.
cook at 250 degrees F. for 10 minutes
change to 275 degrees F. for 15 minutes
change to 300 degrees F. for 15 minutes
change to 350 degrees F. for the remainder of time of about 40 minutes.

Serves 12

Molasses Pound Cake

2/3   cup softened butter or margarine
1/3   cup pulverized raw sugar
2   fertile eggs
2/3   cup unsulfured molasses
2   cups sifted unbleached flour
3/4   teaspoon baking soda
1   teaspoon cinnamon
1/2   teaspoon allspice
1/2   teaspoon nutmeg

Cream the butter and sugar until light and fluffy. Blend in the molasses. Beat in eggs, one at a time. Sift together the flour, baking soda, cinnamon, allspice and nutmeg. Blend this into the molasses mixture. Turn into a greased and floured loaf pan. Bake 45 to 60 minutes in a 350 degrees F. oven until the cake is done. It is done when a toothpick inserted into the center comes out clean. Cool.

Serves 10

Prune-Nut Cake

1   cup chopped pecans
1   cup prunes (cut up, cooked until tender and cooled)
1   cup cold-pressed oil
1½   cups pulverized raw sugar
1½   cups unbleached white flour
1   cup buttermilk
1   teaspoon baking soda
1   teaspoon cinnamon
1   teaspoon allspice
3   fertile eggs
1   teaspoon pure vanilla extract
1/2   teaspoon sea salt
sauce (optional)

129

Cream the oil and sugar. Add the eggs one at a time. Sift the flour, soda, and salt together three times. Add to the creamed mixture alternately with the buttermilk. Begin and end with flour. Add vanilla and spices. Mix well. Fold in nuts and prunes that have had 1 tablespoon flour sprinkled over them. Bake in a greased and lightly floured rectangular cake pan in a 350 degrees F. oven for 30–40 minutes. Pour the sauce over the cake while it is still in the pan. Cut into squares and serve.

Serves 6

Sauce

1/2   cup buttermilk
1   stick butter or soy margarine, softened
1   cup pulverized raw sugar
1   teaspoon natural honey
1/2   teaspoon baking soda
1   teaspoon pure vanilla extract

Mix all the sauce ingredients together in a saucepan. Stir and bring to a boil. Cook 1 minute after mixture comes to a boil.

Pumpkin Bread

Everyone makes banana bread and carrot cake. Why not make pumpkin bread for a change? This is a variation on a recipe belonging to Mrs. Adams, my mother's friend and neighbor.

130

2 cups natural honey
1 cup cold-pressed safflower oil
3 fertile eggs, lightly beaten
2 cups cooked mashed pumpkin
3 cups sifted unbleached white flour or 1½ cups whole
   wheat and 1½ cup unbleached white
3 teaspoons baking powder
2 teaspoons baking soda
1 teaspoon sea salt
1 teaspoon cinnamon
1 teaspoon nutmeg
1/2 cup unsulfured raisins
1 cup chopped pecans

Sift together the dry ingredients. Set aside. In a large mixing bowl add the honey and oil. Cream well and add the eggs one at a time. Add the pumpkin and mix well. Add dry ingredients and mix thoroughly. Pour batter into 2 greased and lightly floured loaf pans. Let stand 20 minutes. Bake in a preheated 350 degrees F. oven for about 1 hour and 30 minutes or until done. Cool and remove from pans.

Each loaf serves 6

Sour Cream Cake

2 sticks margarine at room temperature
3 cups white sugar or pulverized raw sugar
6 large fertile eggs
3 cups unbleached white flour, sifted twice
1 pint sour cream at room temperature
1 teaspoon pure almond extract
1 teaspoon pure vanilla extract

Cream the margarine and the sugar together. Add one egg at a time and mix well. Add the flour alternately with the

sour cream to the creamed mixture. Add the flavorings last.
Bake in a greased and floured tube pan in a 350 degrees F.
oven for about 1½ hours.

Serves 10–12

Spice Cake

2	cups unbleached white flour
1	cup all-purpose whole wheat flour
1	teaspoon sea salt
1	teaspoon baking soda
1	teaspoon cinnamon
1	teaspoon nutmeg
1½	cups pulverized raw sugar
1/2	teaspoon cloves
3	teaspoons baking powder
3/4	cup butter or soy margarine
1	teaspoon pure vanilla extract
3	fertile eggs
1	cup milk
1½	cups peeled, mashed figs (optional)

Sift all dry ingredients together 4 times. Cream the butter;
add the beaten eggs and vanilla. Add the dry sifted ingredients to the creamed mixture. Add the figs and blend well.
Bake in a well-greased lightly floured tube or loaf pan at
350 degrees F. for about 1 hour. If layer pans are used the
baking time will be about 25 minutes. Cake is done when a
toothpick inserted into the center of the cake comes out
clean.

Serves 8–10

Hermits

*A good cookie of unknown origin that has been a fa-
vorite for generations.*

132

1½   cups brown sugar
1   cup butter or soy margarine
2½   cups unbleached flour
1   teaspoon baking soda
2   teaspoons cinnamon
3   well beaten fertile eggs
1/2   teaspoon sea salt
1   cup chopped unsulfured raisins
1   cup currants
1   cup chopped walnuts

Cream the butter and sugar. Sift the flour with the soda, cinnamon, and salt. Add the beaten eggs to the butter and sugar mixture. Add part of the sifted dry ingredients. Mix well. Add raisins, currants, and nuts gradually. Mix well and add the rest of the flour a little at a time. Drop by the teaspoon onto a buttered, floured cookie sheet. Bake in a 300 degrees F. oven for 15 minutes.

Makes 8 dozen

Ganny's Soft Molasses Cookies

6   cups sifted unbleached white flour
1   teaspoon baking powder
1   tablespoon baking soda
1   teaspoon sea salt
1   tablespoon cinnamon
1½   teaspoons ginger
1/4   teaspoon cloves
1   cup solid white shortening or soy margarine
1   cup pulverized raw sugar
1   fertile egg, unbeaten
2   cups unsulfured molasses
1   cup hot water

Sift the flour before measuring. To the 6 cups flour add the baking powder, soda, salt, and spices and sift again. Cream the shortening or margarine and add the sugar gradually, creaming until light and fluffy. Add the egg and molasses

133

and beat well. Mix in the hot water. Chill until firm enough to roll. Roll 1/4″ thick on a lightly floured board. Cut with a floured cutter. Sprinkle with a little pulverized raw sugar. Bake on an ungreased cookie sheet in a 375 degrees F. oven 12–15 minutes or until done.

Makes 50 large cookies

Mammy's Short'n' Bread

It is said that this famous recipe was devised by the mammy in the slave cabin who had to try to make cakes the best she could for her family from limited ingredients. When she could get flour, sugar, and butter this is what she made.

4   cups unbleached flour
1   cup brown sugar
1   cup butter at room temperature

Mix the flour and sugar. Add the butter and cut into the flour mixture well with a fork or pastry blender. Turn out onto a floured surface and pat to 1/2″ thickness. Cut into rectangles or desired shape. Bake in a 325 degrees F. oven 20–25 minutes.

Makes about 2½ dozen cakes

Old Fashioned Tea Cakes

2   cups white or pulverized raw sugar
1   cup butter or soy margarine
1/2   cup buttermilk
3   fertile eggs
1/2   teaspoon baking soda
2   teaspoons baking powder
1   teaspoon pure vanilla extract
Unbleached white flour sufficient to make a soft dough
   (about 5 or 6 cups)

Cream the butter and sugar together. Add the beaten eggs and mix well. Into one cup of flour sift the soda and baking powder. Add this to the sugar mixture. Add the milk and vanilla and enough more flour to make a soft dough. Turn the dough out onto a floured board and knead until smooth. Roll out 1/4" thick. Cut with a circular cutter or other desired shape. Bake in a 350 degrees F. oven until brown and done, about 10 minutes.

Makes 3 dozen cakes

Cooked Sugar (variation of pulled taffy)

The mention of candy making brings fond memories to Mrs. Mildred Smylie of making cooked sugar candy with her mother and sister on cold winter days years ago in Virginia. The children were given jobs pulling bits of the candy after their mother got it started. "You have to pull it and pull it."

3   cups pulverized raw sugar
1/2   cup white vinegar
1/2   cup water

Mix the above ingredients with a spoon in a saucepan until the sugar is mostly dissolved. Boil without stirring until brittle (270 degrees F. on candy thermometer). Pour at once onto a cold buttered marble slab or dish. Cool slightly, just enough to handle. Butter hands and begin pulling candy while hot. Pull until thick. Then twist into a rope shape and place on the marble slab or dish. Cut with kitchen shears at once. Wrap each piece when cooled completely and store in an airtight container. Do not make on a rainy day when the high humidity will interfere with its thickening.

Makes 2 dozen pieces

Mama's Ice Cream

This is good made in an ice cream freezer or in the freezer of the refrigerator. Either way, the word for it is "delightful!"

1   quart milk
4   fertile eggs, separated
1   cup white or pulverized raw sugar
2   teaspoons pure vanilla extract
1   tablespoon unbleached white flour or 1 teaspoon arrowroot

Scald the milk. While the milk is scalding, beat the egg yolks a few strokes. Then gradually beat the sugar and flour or arrowroot into the egg yolks. Strain the scalded milk slowly into the beaten mixture, stirring while pouring. Cook until thick, stirring occasionally. Mixture will lightly coat a wooden spoon. Let cool. Chill for 1–2 hours. Right before freezing add the vanilla and the egg whites which have been stiffly beaten. Fold the whites in gently. Freeze in the ice cream freezer according to the directions for your freezer or pour into refrigerator freezer trays. When the ice cream in the freezer trays starts to thicken around the edges, put it into a bowl and mix it all up and pour back into the trays. Do this once more before it freezes all the way. Strawberries, peaches, or other fresh fruit may be chopped and mixed in after the last beating. To add fruit to the ice cream made in the ice cream freezer add it according to directions with the freezer.

Serves 4–6

Snow Ice Cream

Memories of snowflakes in my childhood are few. Soft fresh snow folded into chilled custard was was a favorite rare treat.

136

1   recipe of MAMA'S ICE CREAM
Clean freshly fallen snow

Prepare the custard and take outside to cool and chill completely. When chilled, but not frozen, bring back inside and quickly fold enough snow into the custard to make an icy treat to be enjoyed immediately.

Makes 1 quart or enough to feed 4 or 5
hungry children

Iron Rich Candy

The high iron content of the fruits gives this delicious treat a nutritional boost.

1/2   lb. honey-dippled dried figs
1/2   lb. unsulfured raisins
1/2   lb. unsulfured dates
1   cup very finely chopped almonds

Chop and mix the three fruits. Pat or roll out the mixture and cut it into pieces. Or it may be just simply rolled into balls. Roll the pieces or balls in the finely chopped almonds. Wrap each piece and store in the refrigerator.

Makes 2½ dozen balls of candy

Molasses Taffy

1   tablespoon butter
1/2   cup pulverized raw sugar
1/4   cup white vinegar
2   cups unsulfured molasses
1   teaspoon baking soda

Dissolve the sugar in the vinegar. Mix in the molasses. Boil until the mixture hardens when dropped from the spoon into cold water (270 degrees F. on the candy thermometer). Then stir in the butter and baking soda. Stir well and pour onto a buttered marble slab or buttered dishes. Pull hard until white (raw sugar will make it a little more honey-colored than refined sugar), using only the buttered finger tips. Lay the long ropes of pulled candy on the dishes and then cut into pieces. Wrap each piece and store in an airtight container.

Makes about 2 dozen pieces

Peanut Brittle

1   cup pulverized raw sugar
1/2   cup water
3   tablespoons natural unfiltered honey
1/3   cup butter or soy margarine
1   cup shelled raw peanuts
1/3   teaspoon sea salt
1   teaspoon pure vanilla extract
1   teaspoon baking soda

Boil sugar, water, and honey for 3 minutes. Add the butter, peanuts, salt, and vanilla. Stir constantly until syrup "clicks" when put in cold water. Peanuts will begin to make popping sounds when it is nearly done. Take off the stove. Beat in the soda quickly. Pour at once onto a buttered cookie sheet. Break into pieces when it has cooled.

Makes 2½ dozen pieces

138

Pralines

Originally pralines were made in France using almonds. This has been a distinctive candy of New Orleans ever since the time the city was settled. Pralines were named after a famous French Marshal, the Duc de Duplessis-Praslin. He believed that almonds coated in sugar would be more digestible. When Louisiana was settled by French colonists they substituted native pecans for almonds. Like many favorite foods there are many recipes for pralines.

2   cups pulverized raw sugar
1   teaspoon baking soda
1   cup buttermilk
1/2   teaspoon sea salt
2   tablespoons butter or soy margarine
1½   cups pecan pieces

Mix together in a saucepan the sugar, soda, buttermilk, and salt. Cook for five minutes over high heat, stirring frequently. Add the butter and cook, stirring until the mixture will form a soft ball when dropped into cold water. Remove from heat. Cool a minute or two. Beat until creamy with an electric beater. Add pecans. Drop by tablespoons at once onto waxed paper. When cool wrap each praline in plastic wrap for storing. Store in an airtight container.

Makes 2 dozen pralines

New Orleans Brown Sugar Pralines

3   cups brown sugar
1/4   cup butter or soy margarine
1   cup cream
1½   cups chopped pecans
1/2   teaspoon pure vanilla extract

Mix together the sugar, butter, and cream and cook until a small quantity dropped into cold water forms a soft ball. Add the chopped pecans and vanilla. Beat with a mixer or by hand until cool. Then drop by spoonfuls onto waxed paper. Pecan halves may be pressed into each praline before hardening if desired. Wrap each praline individually in plastic wrap and store in an airtight container.

Makes 2 dozen

Raisin and Peanut Clusters

1/4   cup unsulfured molasses
1   teaspoon cider vinegar
1/2   cup light honey
3   tablespoons butter or soy margarine
2   cups peanuts, raw or lightly roasted
1   cup seedless raisins

Combine the molasses, honey, and vinegar and cook over a low heat, stirring occasionally until the mixture forms a firm ball when dropped into cold water (250 degrees F. on candy thermometer). Remove from heat and add butter, mixing well. Add the raisins and nuts to the mixture. Drop by teaspoons onto a greased baking sheet. Work quickly. If the mixture begins to harden before all is dropped, reheat the mixture.

Makes 2 dozen clusters

Sugarless Apple Pie

Why do people always make apple pies with such sour apples and then have to add so much sugar? My grandmother made pies from green sour apples from a tree in her yard which were absolutely delicious, but each slice must have contained at least 10 teaspoons sugar. Instead of using sour apples, I use an apple like the Stayman which is just a little tart and requires very little additional sweetening. I think we could even get used to adding no honey very quickly.

pastry for a two-crust pie shell (9")
4   cups fresh apples, peeled, cored, and chopped
1/4   cup toasted wheat germ
1   teaspoon cinnamon
1/2   teaspoon sea salt
2   tablespoons unbleached white flour or 2 teaspoons arrowroot
1   cup homemade applesauce (p. 123) or 1/2 cup apple juice
3   tablespoons butter or soy margarine, cut into pieces
natural honey to sweeten the applesauce to taste

Prepare the bottom crust. Preheat the oven to 375 degrees F. Sweeten the applesauce to taste with natural honey. Dissolve the arrowroot or flour in the juice or mix into the applesauce, stirring until well combined. Combine all other ingredients and then mix in the applesauce or juice mixture. If mixture seems too dry add a little more juice or sauce. Place mixture into the pie shell, piling up the fruit a little in the center. Cover with the top crust and seal edges. Prick top crust to allow steam to escape. If desired glaze the top of the crust with a mixture made by mixing 1 slightly beaten egg white with 1 teaspoon water. Bake at 375 degrees F. for 15 minutes. Then lower the oven to 350 degrees F. for an additional 30–40 minutes or until the apples are tender and the crust browned.

Serves 6

Honey Cream Apple Pie

1/2   cup sour cream
3/4   cup natural honey
1/4   teaspoon sea salt
1   teaspoon cinnamon
1/2   teaspoon nutmeg
6   large tart apples, sliced thin, about 6 cups
pastry for a 2 crust pie shell

Combine the sour cream, honey, salt, and spices. Add the sliced apples and mix well. Line a 9″ pie pan with pastry. Add the apple mixture, heaping the mixture slightly in the center. Top with the remaining crust. Seal and flute the edges of the crust. Prick the top crust with a fork to allow steam to escape. Bake in a hot 425 degrees F. oven 40–45 minutes or until the apples are tender.

Serves 6

Thinking back, we used to get a lot of things free from nature along the country roads when I was a child, everything from Christmas trees to blackberries and wild plums. Along with the blackberries went days of misery from the red bugs, but nevertheless it all seemed like fun. We'd go out and park alongside remote country roads which I thought must have been known only by my daddy. Everyone would go—Mama, Daddy, dogs, and children. We would spend hours filling wash pans with the blackberries to be made later into pies, jelly, and jam. They were mighty good, as I remember, eaten right there on the spot covered with a thin layer of red Mississippi dust!

Blackberry Pie

4   cups fresh blackberries
1   cup pulverized raw sugar or honey to taste for sweetening
2   tablespoons unbleached white flour
4   tablespoons pulverized raw sugar
Pastry for a double 9" pie crust

Wash and remove stems from the berries. Cover with 1 cup sugar and allow to sit for 30 minutes. Combine the flour with the 4 tablespoons sugar and gently stir into the berry-sugar mixture. Spoon into a prepared pastry-lined pie plate. Cover with lattice strips of pastry and bake at 400 degrees F. until the crust is golden brown.

Serves 6

Weidmann's Restaurant

The original Black Bottom Pie recipe included here is claimed by Weidmann's, a unique restaurant in Meridian, Mississippi. Weidmann's was the originator of this Southern specialty some time after the restaurant was opened in 1870 by Felix Weidmann, a Swiss who worked his way to America as a chef on one of the big European ocean liners. It has often been said that Southern cooking cannot be judged by the food served in its restaurants, but instead you must go into the homes to get the real honest-to-goodness Southern food properly prepared. Weidmann's is an exception. Over the generations the Weidmann family has maintained the same high standards, fine foods, excellent service, and genuine hospitality that their predecessors established.

143

Black Bottom Pie

Marvelous!

Crust:

14 ginger snaps
5   tablespoons melted butter or margarine

Crush the ginger snaps by rolling or crushing in the blender. Add the melter butter and pat into a 9" spring pan. Bake in a 425 degrees F. oven 10 minutes. Allow to cool.

Filling:
2   cups scalded milk
4   fertile egg yolks, well beaten
1/2   cup sugar or pulverized raw sugar
1½   tablespoons cornstarch or 1 tablespoon arrowroot
1½   squares bitter chocolate
1   teaspoon pure vanilla extract

Add the eggs *slowly* to the hot milk. Combine and stir into the sugar and cornstarch or arrowroot. Cook in a double boiler for 20 minutes, stirring occasionally, until the mixture coats a spoon (I find that 20 minutes is a lot longer than it actually takes to coat the spoon). Remove from the heat. Take out 1 cup of the custard. To this 1 cup add 1½ squares melted bitter chocolate and beat well as it cools. Add 1 teaspoon pure vanilla extract to the chocolate mixture. Pour the chocolate mixture into the pie crust. Chill while you prepare the next layer.

Second layer:

1   tablespoon gelatin
2   tablespoons cold water
4   stiffly beaten fertile egg whites
1/2   cup sugar or pulverized raw sugar
1/4   teaspoon cream of tartar
2   tablespoons whiskey

Dissolve the gelatin in the cold water. Add remaining custard to the gelatin and cool. Beat the egg whites very stiff with the sugar and cream of tartar. Add the whiskey to the egg whites and then fold into the plain custard mixture. Pour this second layer on top of the chocolate layer. Chill.

Topping:

1   pint heavy whipping cream
a little sugar or pulverized raw sugar to taste
shavings of bitter chocolate

Beat the cream with a little sugar to taste. Right before serving cover the top of the pie with whipped cream. Whip it pretty stiff so it will hold its shape when cut. Top with shavings of bitter chocolate. Remove side of spring pan. Place pie on silver or crystal server.

Serves 8

Note:

The bottom layer of chocolate must be bitter to be the original pie. If, however, you must substitute the sweeter carob powder for the bitter chocolate, use 4 tablespoons carob powder mixed with 3 tablespoons water in place of the melted bitter chocolate.

Plain Pie Pastry

2   cups sifted unbleached white flour
1   teaspoon sea salt
2/3   cup white shortening or margarine
6   tablespoons cold water

Mix the flour and salt together thoroughly. Cut the shortening quickly and carefully into the flour mixture, using a pastry blender. Cut only until the particles of shortening range in size from rice grains to dried beans and each particle is well coated with flour. Add the cold water carefully by sprinkling with one hand while mixing with the other. Use a fork and toss the dampened particles together and to one side. Continue until all particles are moistened and will stick together slightly when pressed gently. Tilt the bowl to one side and shape the mixture into a ball by gently pressing it together. Let rest for 10 minutes. Roll the pastry on a floured board or linen cloth until about 1½ inches larger than the pie pan. Lift gently and fold circle in half over the rolling pin. Lift carefully to the pie pan, placing the folded edge in the center of the pan. Unfold and fit pastry around the sides, stretching a little if necessary. Turn edge of pastry under, even with the edge of the pie plate. Press edges between the tips of the fingers to flute for a one crust pie. If pastry is to have a top crust trim off the excess pastry even with the pie pan and press down with the tines of a fork. If crust is to be precooked, lightly prick the sides and bottom with tines of a fork. Chill the crust to be prebaked if you have time. Bake in a preheated 425 degrees F. oven 12–15 minutes or until crust is delicately browned.

Makes one 9" crust

Two-Crust Pastry

*I always had trouble trying to roll the PLAIN PIE
PASTRY to make two crusts, so if I want a top and a
bottom crust I make one and one-half times the recipe.*

3   cups sifted unbleached white flour
1½   teaspoons sea salt
1   cup shortening or margarine
9   tablespoons cold water

Directions are the same as for the PLAIN PIE PASTRY.

Makes two 9" crusts

Chess Pie

A never-fail version of an old Southern favorite.

4   eggs, beaten
1½   cups pulverized raw sugar
pinch sea salt
2   teaspoons stone ground corn meal
1/4   cup melted butter
4   tablespoons heavy cream
1   teaspoon pure vanilla extract
9"   unbaked pie shell

Cream together well the eggs and sugar. Add all the other
ingredients. Blend well and pour into the unbaked pie shell.
Bake in a 350 degrees F. oven for 30 minutes. Cool.

Serves 6

J.D.'s Coconut Pie

Granddaddy Hughes' favorite of the ones my daddy made for him.

3 fertile eggs, separated
3 tablespoons unbleached white flour or 3 teaspoons arrowroot
3/4 cups white or pulverized raw sugar
1 cup milk
1 tablespoon butter or soy margarine
1 cup freshly grated coconut
pinch of sea salt
1 baked 9" pastry shell

Mix the sugar and flour. Add the milk and the beaten egg yolks. Cook in a double boiler, adding coconut and butter. Cook until the mixture is thickened. Pour into a baked pastry shell and cover with meringue made by stiffly beating 3 egg whites with 2 tablespoons pulverized raw sugar until stiff. Bake in a 350 degrees F. oven until lightly browned. A little coconut added to the meringue before putting it on top of the pie adds a delightful texture.

Serves 6

Egg Custard Pie

3/4 cup pulverized raw sugar
3 yolks and 1 fertile whole egg
1 teaspoon unbleached white flour or 1/3 teaspoon arrowroot
2 cups milk
1/2 teaspoon pure vanilla extract
2 fertile egg whites for meringue
1 unbaked pie shell (9")
1 teaspoon pulverized raw sugar for meringue

Beat the sugar and 3 yolks and 1 whole egg together well. Add the arrowroot or flour, milk, and vanilla mixing well.

148

Pour the mixture into an uncooked 9" pie shell and bake at 400 degrees F. until set. A silver knife will come out clean when inserted into the custard. Make the meringue with the other 2 egg whites and 1 teaspoon pulverized raw sugar until they form stiff peaks. Put the meringue on top of the pie and put back into the oven to brown the meringue. Cool and serve.

Serves 6

Easy Lemon Pie

1 9" unbaked pie shell
1 cup pulverized raw sugar
2 tablespoons butter or soy margarine
2 tablespoons unbleached flour
2 egg yolks from fertile eggs
1 cup milk
8 tablespoons lemon juice
2 beaten fertile egg whites

Cream the sugar and butter. Add the flour and mix. Add yolks. Beat until smooth. Add milk and juice. Fold in the beaten egg whites. Pour into an unbaked pie shell. Bake 10 minutes at 350 degrees F. and then 40 minutes at 325 degrees F.

Serves 6

Macaroon Pie

15 plain soda crackers
15 unsulfured dates, chopped
1 cup raw pulverized sugar (less sugar could be added according to taste)
1/4 teaspoon baking powder
3 egg whites, stiffly beaten
1 teaspoon pure almond extract
1/2 cup chopped pecans
1 pint whipped cream

149

Crumble crackers finely and add all other ingredients to the crackers. Fold in the beaten egg whites. Put into a greased pie pan and bake in a 275 degrees F. oven for 30 minutes. Slice and serve slightly warm or cool. Top with whipped cream.

Serves 6

Orange Pie

1   cup pulverized raw sugar or white sugar
4   fertile eggs, separated
pinch sea salt
1½   teaspoons gelatin
juice of 1 lemon
juice of 1 orange
grated rind of 1 orange
1   cup graham cracker crumbs
1/2   stick melted butter or soy margarine
1   pint heavy cream (optional)

Make a graham cracker crust by mixing together the crumbs made in the blender with the melted butter or margarine in a bowl. Press the crust mixture on the bottom and up towards the sides of a spring form pan. Cook 10 minutes in a 350 degrees F. oven. Cool. Beat the egg yolks. Add the lemon and orange juices, orange rind, salt, and 1/2 cup of the sugar. Cook until thick in a double boiler. Add to the cooked mixture the gelatin that has been soaked 10 minutes in 1/2 cup cold water. Beat the egg whites with the remaining sugar until stiff. Fold into the cooked mixture. Pour into the crust and chill in the refrigerator until firm, about 2 hours. Serve with whipped cream spooned on top of each piece if desired.

Serves 6

Peach Cobbler

"The first cobbler our Southern cooks made in such perfection," claims a crumbling 1908 Good Housekeeper's Cook Book. *It continues, "A real old fashioned cook is a stickler for a few spoonfuls of brandy poured over the peaches before the top crust is put on, but the majority of folk find it quite delectable enough without any spirituous additions."*

Butter a deep earthenware pudding dish or Pyrex baking dish at least 3½" deep. Line the sides with pie pastry. Then fill the dish with peeled peaches cut into slices. Sweeten with molasses or sugar to taste if you wish. Cover with a layer of top crust, sealing it down so that none of the juices may escape. Bake in a 400 degrees F. oven, about 45 minutes. If the cobbler seems to be browning too much lower the heat.

Serves 6

Peach Pie

Good and easy, this pie can be made with other fruits such as pears, cherries, or apples. The batter will rise up through the fruit and make a nice top crust when baked.

2   cups peeled and sliced peaches
2/3   cup pulverized sugar (or 1/2 cup natural honey)
2/3   cup unbleached white flour
2   teaspoons baking powder
2/3   cup milk
3/4   stick melted butter or soy margarine
1/4   cup water
      square baking dish

151

Melt the butter in the square baking dish in a 350 degrees F. oven. Mix together the sugar or honey, flour, baking powder, and milk. Pour this batter over the melted butter in the dish. Heat the fruit with 1/4 cup water and spoon the fruit on top of the batter. Bake at 350 degrees F. for about 30 minutes until brown.

Serves 6

J.D.'s Pecan Pie

"Pecan" is an Indian word originating from pacan *used by the Indians to designate all nuts hard enough to require a stone to crack them. This first pecan pie was my daddy's recipe. It contains corn syrup, however, so if you would rather not use the refined corn syrup, try one of my own two that follow using honey or brown sugar.*

4   fertile eggs, slightly beaten
1   cup sugar or pulverized raw sugar
1   cup corn syrup
1/8 teaspoon sea salt
1½   teaspoons pure vanilla extract
3   tablespoons butter, melted
1   cup pecan halves
9"   unbaked pie shell

Preheat the oven to 350 degrees F. Mix together the eggs, sugar, and corn syrup. Add the other ingredients. Pour the mixture into an unbaked 9" pie shell. Bake at 350 degrees F. until a silver knife inserted into the mixture comes out clean, about 1 hour. Cool before serving. This is delicious served with a scoop of natural vanilla ice cream on top.

Serves 6

Brown Sugar Pecan Pie

Nothing is more Southern than a pecan pie. Although most people make them with corn syrup, this one using brown sugar instead is just as good.

3   fertile eggs, slightly beaten
2   cups brown sugar
1   stick butter or soy margarine, softened
1½   teaspoons pure vanilla extract
1   cup chopped pecan pieces
1   9″ unbaked pie shell
1/8   teaspoon sea salt

Cream together the eggs and the brown sugar. Cream into that mixture the softened butter. Add the vanilla, pecans, and salt. Pour the mixture into the unbaked pie shell. This recipe makes a lot of filling so if your crust is not very deep this mixture could make two pies. Fill the pie shells about 2/3 of the way up. Bake in a preheated 350 degrees F. oven for 40 minutes or until the pie is almost set. Lower the heat to 250 degrees F. for about 15 minutes longer.

Serves 6

Honey Pecan Pie

4   fertile eggs
1   cup pulverized raw sugar
1   cup light natural honey such as orange or alfalfa
1/8   teaspoon sea salt
1½   teaspoons pure vanilla extract
3   tablespoons butter or soy margarine, melted
1   cup pecans, each half chopped into 6 or 7 pieces
1   9″ unbaked pie shell

153

Mix the eggs and sugar together, creaming well. Add the honey and other ingredients. Mix. Pour the mixture into the unbaked pie shell and bake at 350 degrees F. for about an hour or until a knife inserted into the mixture comes out clean.

Serves 6

Ganny's Sweet Potato Pie

I never got tired of eating this at Ganny's. For some reason the sweet potatoes I buy just don't seem to taste as good as hers did.

2   cups cooked mashed sweet potatoes
3/4   cup light brown sugar, firmly packed or pulverized raw sugar
2   fertile eggs, slightly beaten
2   cups milk
3   tablespoons melted butter or soy margarine
1   teaspoon cinnamon
3/4   teaspoon ginger
1/2   teaspoon nutmeg
3/4   teaspoon sea salt
9"   unbaked pie shell

Preheat the oven to 425 degrees F. Mix together the potatoes, sugar, eggs, milk and butter (or margarine). Add the spices. Mix and pour into the unbaked pie crust. Bake in a 425 degrees F. oven for about 1 hour. Ganny says to bake "until it looks done." That translated means until the pie is set and lightly browned on top.

Serves 6

Sliced Sweet Potato Pie

"I don't care what you have to eat, I always want something sweet." My grandfather Hughes' quote expresses the feelings of most Southerners. This pie is one of his favorites.

2 medium sized sweet potatoes
1 cup pulverized raw sugar
1/2 cup butter or soy margarine, melted
1 cup boiling water
1 teaspoon cinnamon
1 teaspoon cloves and allspice mixed
juice and grated rinds of 2 lemons (optional)
pastry

Peel and parboil the sweet potatoes. Slice them and put into a deep pie plate that has been lined with pastry. Pour over the potatoes a sauce made from mixing all the other ingredients. Cover with a top crust. Join edges together. Bake in a 350 degrees F. oven about an hour until potatoes are completely done.

Serves 6

Octa's Baked Custard

This is the handwritten recipe from a faded composition book belonging to a friend. Octa was her mother's cook in Virginia years ago.

3 fertile eggs, beaten lightly
3/4 cup pulverized raw sugar
2 cups milk
1 teaspoon pure vanilla extract
nutmeg

155

Combine the beaten eggs and the sugar. Add the milk and vanilla. Mix well. Pour into a shallow dish or individual custard cups and set in a pan of hot water. Sprinkle with nutmeg and bake at 325 degrees F. until firm. Do not let the water around the cups reach the boiling point.

Serves 4

Old Fashioned Baked Custard

This contains less sugar than Octa's recipe.

2   cups milk
3   fertile eggs
5   tablespoons pulverized raw sugar
2   tablespoons cold water
grating of nutmeg

Heat the milk. Do not let it boil. Beat the eggs and add the sugar with the water. Stir rapidly into the heated mixture. Mix well. Pour into custard cups and sprinkle with freshly grated nutmeg. Place cups in a pan surrounded with an inch and a half of water and bake in a 325 degree F. oven until well set. Do not let the water around the cups reach the boiling point.

Serves 4

Grapenuts Custard

A delicious simple variation to a baked custard recipe is made by sprinkling into the bottom of each dish a few uncooked grapenuts. Then pour the custard in and cook as directed.

Banana Pudding

3/4   cup pulverized raw sugar
1   cup milk
2   fertile eggs
2   tablespoons unbleached white flour or arrowroot
pinch sea salt
pinch baking powder
3   extra fertile egg whites for meringue
3   ripe bananas
vanilla wafers or leftover pound cake

Mix the flour or arrowroot, sugar, salt, and baking powder. Add the milk, mixing well. Beat the 2 eggs and mix with the other mixture. Cook until thick in the top of a double boiler. Line a Pyrex dish with vanilla wafers or pound cake cut into rectangular pieces. Then cover with a layer of bananas. Pour over this part of the cooked custard. Repeat until the dish is full, letting a layer of wafers or cake cover the top. Top with meringue made by stiffly beating the extra 3 egg whites with sugar to taste. Bake in a 350 degrees F. oven just until the meringue browns lightly. Cool before serving. To fill a deep dish double the recipe.

Serves 6

Ganny's Coconut Pudding

Good and easy.

1   cup pulverized raw sugar
1   tablespoon unbleached flour
3   fertile eggs
1   cup milk
1   tablespoon butter or soy margarine, melted
1   teaspoon pure vanilla extract
1   cup freshly grated coconut

157

Mix the sugar and flour together. Add the eggs and blend well. Add the milk and the remaining ingredients. Pour the pudding into a greased Pyrex dish. Cook at 325 degrees F. until set and firm for about 30 minutes.

Serves 6

Honey-Apple Pudding

1   fertile egg beaten until thick and lemon colored
2/3   cup natural honey
1/3   cup whole wheat flour
1/4   teaspoon sea salt
1½   teaspoons baking powder
1   cup raw apples, peeled and chopped
1/2   cup chopped pecans or black walnuts
pint heavy cream, whipped and sweetened to taste

Gradually add the honey to the beaten egg. Sift the flour, salt, and baking powder together. Add to the egg mixture. Fold in the chopped apples and nuts. Pour into a well buttered pie pan. Bake in a 350 degrees F. oven for 30 minutes or until crisp. Top with whipped cream.

Serves 6

Cooked Fruit

Stewed fresh fruit is a good accompaniment with meat or as a nutritious dessert.

Apples, peaches and pears should be washed, cut in pieces, pared, cored or stoned before being stewed. Berries need only to be washed and sorted. Rhubarb, which is not a fruit, but is used in place of one, should be washed and cut into small pieces. If the skin is tough, peel it off before cutting the rhubarb up. Cherries are often cooked without

158

being stoned. To cook fruits, add only enough water to keep them from scorching. Cook them gently until they are tender and sweeten to taste with natural honey or pulverized raw sugar.

Allow 1/2 cup cooked fruit per serving

Honey-Baked Apples

With their spicy flavor these apples are good served with any roast or main dish, as a garnish, or as a side dish.

4   medium apples
2   tablespoons water
1/2   cup natural honey
1½   teaspoons cinnamon
3   tablespoons butter or soy margarine

Core the apples. Do not peel. Cut them into fourths. Arrange the apples in a shallow, buttered baking dish. Combine the honey and spices. Pour over the apples. Dot with butter. Pour water around the apples in the dish. Bake in a 350 degrees F. oven for 30–40 minutes or until the apples are tender. Baste occasionally with syrup. Serve warm with cream if desired.

Serves 4

Prune Whip

The chopped nuts added to this dessert give a different taste to an old favorite.

1½   cups pitted mashed cooked prunes
1/4   cup pulverized raw sugar or natural honey
1   teaspoon lemon juice
1/2   cup whipping cream
1   fertile egg white
pinch of sea salt
1/4   cup finely chopped blanched almonds

Whip the cream and egg white separately until stiff. Combine the cream and egg white. Blend in the sweetening, salt, and juice. Add prunes in small amounts and beat thoroughly with each addition. Stir the almonds into the prune whip mixture. Place the prune whip in individual dishes and chill well before serving.

Serves 4

DRINKS AND PUNCHES

The South's sultry weather and its informal way of life provide many occasions when a hostess needs cool drinks and punches. Sugar-frosted glasses are a perfect complement for cooling summer drinks. Just brush the rims of the glasses with a little beaten egg white and then dip them into a shallow dish containing confectioners' sugar. Or the rims may be dipped into lemon juice, then in sugar. Chill the glasses in the refrigerator. When ready to use fill them carefully with the beverage.

Garnish cool drinks with a lemon, lime, or orange slice, a sprig of mint, or a cherry, strawberry, or other piece of fruit. Even the most weary and warm guest will brighten after such sparkling refreshment.

Iced tea is the standard everyday beverage year-round. Most people still brew their own and do not use the instant teas. Fresh mint has long been a flavorful addition to tea and a variety of other beverages. If fresh mint is not available it can be bought in dried flakes and leaves and used in beverages for the flavor, but the beauty of the fresh sprigs as garnishes cannot be imitated.

Teas and coffees are given in the South for almost any occasion. Fresh-cut flowers from the garden accompany gleaming silver services proudly displayed and surrounded by tiny sandwiches and pastries. Such a mid-afternoon tea for a young bride-to-be or other honored person is a charming affair that again reflects the relaxed, but well-planned, approach to special occasions that is enjoyed by all in the South.

Berry Acid

Berries were made into concentrated mixtures before the day of freezers called "acids" or "shrubs." The "acid" was diluted and used as a basis for fruit punches or cool drinks. This was considered a particularly fine beverage for picnics.

12 lbs. berries (blackberries or raspberries)
2   quarts water
5   ounces tartaric acid or 1/2 cup freshly squeezed lemon
    juice
pulverized raw sugar or natural honey for sweetening to
    taste

Wash the berries, discarding any that are not perfect. Put the berries in a pan and cover with the water which has previously been acidulated with the tartaric acid or lemon juice. Let stand 48 hours. Then strain or let drip through a cheesecloth bag, squeezing hard enough to get all the juice out. To each pint of juice add 1 lb. pulverized raw sugar or honey (or less according to taste). Stir until dissolved and cook 5 minutes. Bottle and cork tightly. Keep in a cool place. Put 1/4 cup of the acid into a glass. Add water and crushed ice. Serve immediately.

Serves about 20

Carob Syrup

Nature's most perfect beverage of course is milk. Children need 3 or 4 cups of milk each day and adults need at least 2 cups. Chocolate syrup has long been a favorite flavoring for milk. Some now prefer carob to chocolate because it contains natural sweetness and does not cause the allergic reactions that chocolate does in some people. A commercial version of this syrup is available in health food stores.

1 cup carob powder
1¼ cups water
1/2 cup light natural honey
1 teaspoon pure vanilla extract

Slowly add the water to the carob powder, mixing well. Add the honey. Bring to a boil and boil 2 or 3 minutes, stirring while it cooks. Cool and add vanilla. Refrigerate and use like chocolate syrup as needed. Use 1 to 2 tablespoons for a glass of milk.

Makes 1½ cups

Hot Cider

1 gallon sweet cider
juice of 4 oranges
juice of 4 lemons
1/2 teaspoon nutmeg
2 teaspoons ground allspice
1 teaspoon ground cinnamon
4 sticks whole cinnamon
2 cups pulverized raw sugar (or less according to taste)

Mix together the cider, fruit juices and sugar. Tie the nutmeg, allspice, and ground cinnamon in a cheesecloth bag. Add the bag to the liquids and boil 2 or 3 minutes. Remove the bag and float cinnamon sticks on top. Serve hot.

Serves 25

Mulled Cider

1 gallon sweet cider
1 tablespoon whole cloves
6 sticks cinnamon, broken into pieces
1 tablespoon whole allspice
2 pieces whole mace
brown sugar to taste
2½ cups spiced crab apples

Put the cider into a large pot. Add the cinnamon. Tie the other spices in a cheesecloth bag and put into cider. Stir in the brown sugar. Heat and simmer 20 minutes. Add the apples during the last 5 minutes of cooking time. Before serving remove the spice bag. Serve hot with a crab apple in each cup.

Serves 6–7

Iced Tea

4 cups boiling water
4 teaspoons tea
pulverized raw sugar or honey to taste
lemon slices and sprigs of mint for garnishes

Pour the boiling water over the tea. Cover and steep 5 minutes. Strain. Cool and sweeten to taste. Pour over ice, diluting a little if desired. Garnish with lemon slices and mint.

Serves 4

Fruit Waters

Fruit waters like "acids" are concentrated fruit juices used to make cool drinks.

4   tall chilled glasses
1   quart chilled ginger ale or sparkling water
1   cup fresh currants or berries
1/4   cup water
1/4   cup pulverized raw sugar or natural honey
1/8   teaspoon cinnamon

Rinse, drain, and discard any stems from the currants. Place the currants in a saucepan with the water. Cover and simmer 10 minutes. Remove from heat. Force the currants through a sieve to remove any seeds. Blend into the mixture the sugar or honey and cinnamon. Chill the mixture thoroughly in the refrigerator. To serve pour equal amounts of syrup into the 4 glasses. Fill with ginger ale or sparkling water. It may be served over ice. Serve at once. *Variation:* Fill the glasses 2/3 full with ginger ale or sparkling water, dividing the syrup equally as before. Float a scoop of ice cream in each glass.

Serves 4

Quick Modern Fruit Waters

1   quart ginger ale or sparkling water
1   12 oz. can frozen fruit juice concentrate

Concentrated frozen fruit juices such as orange, orange and grapefruit, or grape can be reconstituted with ginger ale or sparkling water instead of water. Mix together thawed juice and the ginger ale or sparkling water and serve over ice.

Serves 4–6

Mama's Fruit Punch

This is the punch I remember my mama making for our birthday parties as a child. It uses natural fruit juices and is delicious for any occasion or age group.

4   quarts carbonated water
2   cups crushed pineapple without heavy syrup if available (If you can't find this crushed without heavy syrup, buy the slices packed in their own juice and put fruit and juice in the blender for a few seconds just until crushed up, not liquefied.)
2   quarts grape juice
2   lbs. pulverized raw sugar (or less according to taste)
3   cups fresh squeezed orange juice
1   cup fresh squeezed lemon juice

Boil 1 quart water and the sugar for 1 minute. Cool. Add all the fruits and juices. This much may be made ahead of time. Add the carbonated water right before serving. Serve in a punch bowl with ice cubes. Garnish with orange and lemon slices, and sprigs of fresh mint from the garden. Use one of the naturally carbonated waters if available.

Serves 25–30

Lemon Ginger Punch

Many Southern punches have a citrus fruit base. The older boys (no age limit) like this!

5   lemons
1   quart water
1   cup pulverized raw sugar or natural honey
1   quart ginger ale or sparkling water
several sprigs fresh mint

Make an unusually strong lemonade by mixing the juice of 5 lemons with the water and sugar. Mix until sugar is dissolved. Put over ice in a large punch bowl. Right before serving add and mix in the ginger ale. Bruise the stems and leaves of the mint and add to the punch bowl. Garnishes of lemon and orange slices may also be added.

Serves 8

Hot Lemonade

1/2   fresh lemon
hot water
pulverized raw sugar or honey to taste

Squeeze the juice of the lemon into a glass. Put a spoon in the glass to keep it from cracking. Then fill it up with hot water and sweeten to taste.

Serves 1

Cold Lemonade

The South probably uses more lemonade in the summer than any other section of the country.

Use the same ingredients and amounts as for HOT LEMONADE, except use cold water and fill the glasses with ice cubes. Garnish with sprigs of mint and lemon slices.

Serves 1

Spiced Lemonade

Freeze whole cloves or mint or lemon slices in ice cubes to add appeal to this summertime favorite.

6   lemons, juiced
4   cups water
10   whole cloves
3/4 cup pulverized raw sugar or honey to taste
3/4   cup water

Boil the 3/4 cup raw sugar or honey in 3/4 cup water about 5 minutes. Measure 1 cup of the syrup and cook an additional 5 minutes with the cloves. Strain the syrup. Add the juice of the lemons and the 4 cups water. Chill. Pour over ice cubes and serve.

Serves 6

Mint Fruit Punch

6   large sprigs mint
2   quarts boiling water
2   cups freshly squeezed orange juice
2   cups pineapple juice
1   cup freshly squeezed lemon juice
1½   quarts 7-Up or sparkling water

Add the boiling water to the mint and let steep 10 minutes. Strain. Mix in the fruit juices. Add the sparkling water just before serving. Serve from an ice-filled punch bowl. Garnish with mint and fruit slices.

Serves 16

North Carolina Syllabub

A rich pep-up drink

1   pint cream
1/2 cup milk
1/2 cup sweet cider
1/2 teaspoon pure vanilla extract
1/2 cup pulverized raw sugar or honey to taste
pinch nutmeg
1   tablespoon sherry (optional)

Chill all the ingredients. Mix all ingredients in a mixing bowl except the cream. Beat the cream lightly and add to the other ingredients and beat lightly. Sprinkle a little nutmeg on top and *serve immediately*. Whiskey or brandy may be used instead of the cider.

Serves 6

Orangeade

6   cups freshly squeezed orange juice
1/4 cup freshly squeezed lemon juice
2   cups water
1½ cups pulverized raw sugar or honey to taste

Mix all the ingredients together and chill thoroughly. Stir again and pour over ice cubes or crushed ice.

Serves 8

Plantation Mint Tea Drink

2 cups pulverized raw sugar or natural honey to taste
2 cups water or 1½ cups water if honey is used
juice of 4 lemons
2 cups hot strong tea
2 cups crushed fresh mint leaves

Let the sugar and water come to a boil in a saucepan. Mix with the lemon juice. Pour tea over the mint leaves. Let stand until cooled. Strain and pour into syrup and lemon juice mixture. Pour into glasses half filled with finely crushed ice. Garnish with sprigs of mint.

Serves 12

Temperance Mint Julep

This is made without spirits.

1 cup loosely filled with mint sprigs
juice of 2 lemons
grated rind of 1 lemon
2 cups water
1 lb. pulverized raw sugar
juice of 1 orange
pineapple juice equal in quantity to the orange juice
wine glasses
sprigs of mint and a strawberry to garnish each drink

Crush the mint, rubbing each leaf with a wooden mallet. Then soak mint 30 minutes in the lemon juice and lemon rind. Cook together the water and sugar until the syrup spins a thread. Take from the fire and stir the mixture into the lemon and mint. Add the orange and pineapple juice. Strain and put into the refrigerator to chill well. Serve in wine glasses with a sprig of mint and a berry on top of the glass. It may be served over crushed ice.

Serves 6–8

CHRISTMAS AND OTHER HOLIDAYS

The Southern colonists had both religious and folk celebrations of Christmas in the seventeenth and eighteenth
centuries. The colonists who celebrated Christmas from
England, Holland, and Germany emphasized eating, drinking, family gatherings and joyousness at the Christmas season. It just never seemed to bother the Southerner that by
Puritan standards the way he celebrated Christmas might
be more pagan than Christian. He was having too much fun
to notice!

Virginia was settled by the Church of England colonists
who emphasized the folk quality of Christmas even though
they regarded the birth of Christ as a Holy Day. Christmas
was regarded as a season beginning well before December
25th and lasting until January 6th. Usually the Christmas
tree in the South is down by New Year's Day. Even today
in Williamsburg, Virginia, one of their ceremonies includes
the burning of a bonfire of discarded Christmas trees at twi-
light on New Year's Day which symbolized the old super-
stition that it is bad luck to have the tree up after New
Year's Day.

171

Tipsy Cake

This is an old Virginia recipe that was traditional at Christmas and New Year's dinners in the home of the Warner family of Springfield. Tipsy cake is beautiful and well worth the preparation. The base is a sponge cake into which are stuck blanched almonds. It is then drizzled with dry drinking sherry and covered with cold custard and syllabub right before serving.

The Sponge Cake

6   fertile eggs, separated
1½   cups white or pulverized raw sugar
1½   cups sifted unbleached white flour
1/2 teaspoon sea salt
6   tablespoons cold water
1   teaspoon grated lemon rind
1   teaspoon lemon extract
1½   teaspoons baking powder

Beat the egg yolks until thick and lemon colored. Beat in the sugar gradually. Sift the flour and salt together and add alternately with the water to the first mixture. Add the lemon extract and rind. Whip the egg whites until foamy. Add baking powder and continue whipping until stiff peaks are formed. Fold into the egg yolk mixture. Pour into an ungreased tube cake pan. Cook 35 minutes in a 350 degrees F. oven with a pan of water over it on the rack above. Then take the water out and bake 10–15 minutes without the pan of water until done. Invert to cool. This makes a big puffy angel-type cake. When the cake is cooled remove from the pan and put onto a large cake plate. Custard mixture and cream will ooze down the sides of the cake and collect around the cake on the plate. Stick blanched, split or whole, almonds into the cake. Drizzle dry drinking sherry over the cake. Use this to taste, but not enough to make the cake soggy. (This much may be prepared ahead of serving.) The following should be done as near serving time as possible. Cover the cake with cold, but not frozen, custard made the day before.

Custard for Tipsy Cake

4 cups milk
1/2 cup white or pulverized raw sugar
6 fertile egg yolks
pinch sea salt
1 teaspoon pure vanilla extract

Scald the milk. Beat egg yolks until light and lemon colored. Add the sugar and salt. Pour scalded milk over the beaten egg mixture, a little at a time. Strain this mixture into the top of a double boiler. Cook over simmering water until the mixture coats a spoon. Remove from heat and cool. Add vanilla. Chill this in the refrigerator overnight or until to be used. Cover the Tipsy Cake with the cold custard. Then cover the custard with the syllabub which in this recipe is simply cream whipped with a wire whip just until bubbles remain before it really starts to get thick. Cut and serve at once, spooning some of the custard and syllabub from the cake plate onto each serving.

Serves 10–12

Where did the Christmas tree first appear in America? There is an account of one at Fort Dearborn, Michigan, in 1804 and it is probable that they appeared before the 1840s in rural Pennsylvania settled by the Germans. Perhaps the most popular story is of the Christmas tree and Charles Minnegerode, a German professor at William and Mary College in Williamsburg, Virginia. Professor Minnegerode introduced the custom from his native Germany in 1842 in the home of the elderly Judge Nathaniel Beverly Tucker. The excitement spread to the neighbors and in time through the whole town. From there it spread from Williamsburg to other places in Virginia and eventually throughout the entire South. In Mississippi the diary of Mrs. Mahala Eggleston Roach, a niece of Jefferson Davis, tells that she introduced the Christmas tree in the Vicksburg area in 1851.

History shows that Richmond was perhaps the place of the first store window display at Christmas. In the mid 1840s Mr. August Bodeker of Richmond facing his first Christmas away from the Old Country in a strange land set up a tree in the front of his store and decorated it with candles and ornaments. So the spirit of Christmas spread rapidly through the Southern States where it became the biggest holiday of the year.

Christmas couldn't help but become the South's most popular holiday season with its developing emphasis on family gatherings and parties. Without your family with you on Christmas there is no real joy even in the presence of the religious emphasis. Religion is important to the Southerner, but the real Christmas celebrations are felt in the family closeness and the joy of the children.

Eggnog

Exchanges of hospitality mark the beginning of the Christmas holiday season ahead. Eggnog parties play a prominent part. This is an old Southern way of saying "happy holiday." There are many good eggnog recipes, but this is a favorite. It is really quite simple to prepare and has no resemblence to the so-called eggnog sold in cartons around the holiday today.

12 fertile eggs, separated
12 tablespoons white or pulverized raw sugar
3/4 cup Bourbon (optional or to taste)
1 quart cream, whipped
12 stiffly beaten egg whites from the fertile eggs
1 pint natural ingredients vanilla ice cream

Beat the egg yolks until thick and lemon colored. Add the sugar gradually. Add the Bourbon by the spoonfuls *slowly*. Fold in the whipped cream. *Fold* in the stiffly beaten egg whites. Add the ice cream, *folding gently*. If this should be too thick add a little milk. Prepare the eggnog in the punch bowl and serve immediately into individual cups. Serve with fruit cake, nuts, or other Christmas time treats.

Serves 20

Charlotte Russe

Simply a cream mixture molded with cake on the outside.

1   quart milk
4   fertile egg yolks
1   pint whipping cream
3/4   teaspoon pure vanilla extract
1   cup white or pulverized raw sugar
2   envelopes gelatin
1/4   teaspoon pure almond extract
ladyfingers for lining mold

First line the bottom of a straight-sided mold with oiled brown paper. Then arrange ladyfingers evenly around the side. Combine half of the sugar with the milk and scald. Beat the egg yolks with 1/4 cup sugar until light. Add a small amount of hot milk, then pour all into the milk and sugar mixture stirring constantly. Cook in a double boiler about 3 minutes or until the mixture coats the spoon. Remove from the heat and add the gelatin which has been softened with 1/4 cup cold water. Stir until thoroughly dissolved. When custard is cold and begins to set gently fold in the cream which has been whipped and sweetened with the remaining sugar. Pour into the lined mold. Chill until firm. Unmold by dipping the mold into warm water and inverting onto a platter or flat dish. Serve with additional whipped cream if desired.

Serves 10

Each Christmas holds its own special memories of smells, tastes, and impressions. To the child of the 1800s it might have been the smell and taste of the orange, a delicacy. They were something special and even after the Civil War every family somehow still managed to buy an orange to drop into the children's stockings. The oranges were shared among other family members and the peels were kept for flavoring cakes or other sweets.

Ambrosia

This paradisiacal treat is made from two former rarities in the South—oranges and coconuts—combined and sugared the previous day and their flavors allowed to mingle overnight. Ambrosia is traditionally served at the Christmas dinner.

6   large oranges that peel easily
1   cup grated fresh coconut (see glossary, page 7, for preparation)

Peel and skin the oranges. Separate into sections. Cut down each side of the section on the inside of the membrane toward the center and lift out the section. Sections may be cut in thirds or left whole as desired. Place in a large bowl. Add sugar or honey to taste and stir. Stir in the grated coconut, saving enough to sprinkle on the tops of individual servings later. Place bowl in refrigerator and chill overnight. Serve in sherbet glasses and top with coconut.

Serves 6

Candied Orange Peel

This is Ganny's recipe and one of our Christmas favorites.

176

peel of 4 medium oranges
1   cup pulverized raw sugar
water

Remove peel in quarters and pick off any stringy fibers. Wash well. Scrape off dark sections on outside skin. Cover with cold water. Bring to a boil and cook until the peel is tender. Remove peel, strain water, and save 1/2 cup. Add sugar to the orange water and boil until it forms a soft ball in water. While syrup is cooking, cut the peel with scissors in pieces lengthwise in eighths or smaller. Drop peel into syrup when it reaches the soft ball stage and cook slowly until the peel is clear looking or syrup forms a long thread. Stir to prevent scorching. Remove peel or drain syrup and drop each piece of peel separately into finely pulverized raw sugar (or white), coating each piece well. Shake off excess sugar and lay each piece on waxed paper to cool and dry.

Candied Grapefruit or Lemon Peel

Same as for orange peel, except these should be boiled in larger quantities of water, beginning with cold water. Change water one or two times, as preferred. Fresh water is used to make syrup.

For others Christmas meant the season for hunting game. But for all and above all it was a season of warm family gatherings unequaled anywhere for its festivity and hospitality. Christmas is the time when Southern cooking comes into its own. In the Virginia Colony it began as English cooking with turkey, venison, and oysters replacing the English dish of boar's head and peacock. There was throughout the South of course a mixture of ethnic influences in the cooking. These ranged from the English of Virginia to the French in Florida and Louisiana to the Ger-

177

mans in several states. All of this merged into a unique cooking. In antebellum days the slaves and the mistress of the house began the preparation of the Christmas food weeks and weeks before.

Creamed Oysters in Patty Shells

Delicious for hors d'oeuvre for a special holiday meal.

Tiny little cooked patty shells
1   oyster for each patty shell
1/2   teaspoon butter or soy margarine for each oyster
pinch of sea salt for each oyster
pinch cayenne

Stew the oysters in their own liquor until plump and the edges ruffled. Add the other ingredients to the oysters to make a cream mixture. Serve from a chafing dish and spoon into the patty shells right before serving.

Allow 5 or 6 per person

Christmas Turkey

Although Benjamin Franklin lost his campaign to elect the American wild turkey as the national bird, the turkey, its varieties now domesticated, has gained national recognition as the "Christmas Bird." The wild turkey was first eaten by English settlers in Virginia.

Turkey may be stuffed with MAMA'S CHRISTMAS TURKEY DRESSING (p. 179), or it may be cooked unstuffed and the dressing cooked separately in a casserole. Allow about 3/4 lb. per person for a generous serving for turkeys weighing less than 12 lbs. Over 12 lbs., allow 1/2 lb. per serving. Clean the turkey thoroughly. Salt the inside of the cavity. Fill the cavity loosely with the dressing. Sew or skewer the opening shut. Tie the drumsticks securely to the tail. Brush the skin with melted butter. Cover the turkey with a tent of aluminum foil. Baste the turkey with more melted butter several times during roasting. When it is about half-done, cut the leg strings for the rest of the cooking time. The turkey is done when the leg joints move easily and when the juices do not run red when a fork is pushed deep into the thickest part of the meat. If using a meat thermometer it should reach a reading of 185 degrees F. placed in the center of the inside thigh muscle or in the center of the thickest meaty part. Remove tent to finish browning for the last 30 minutes of cooking time.

Roasting times for whole chilled turkeys
325 degrees F.
(allow 5 min. per lb. extra for stuffed turkeys)

8 to 12 lbs.	4 to 4½ hours
12 to 16 lbs.	4½ to 5 hours
16 to 20 lbs.	5½ to 7 hours
20 to 24 lbs.	7 to 8½ hours

Mama's Christmas Turkey Dressing

3   cups biscuit crumbs
2   cups corn bread crumbs (all or mostly all 5 cups may be corn bread crumbs)
2   fertile eggs, slightly beaten
2¼ cups liquid (half hot water, half broth)
2   tablespoons melted butter or soy margarine
1   tablespoon minced parsley
2   teaspoons chopped sweet green pepper
1/4 cup chopped celery
1/4 cup chopped onion
1/2 teaspoon sea salt
1/2 teaspoon freshly ground black pepper
1/4 teaspoon sweet marjoram or 1/2 teaspoon sage
1/2 teaspoon baking powder

Add the seasonings to the breads. Add the liquid. Let stand about an hour. Now add the slightly beaten eggs. Blend in the baking powder and turn the dressing into a large greased casserole. Bake covered 20 minutes, then uncovered 20 minutes at 350 degrees F. If you want to use this dressing to stuff a turkey, you may have to double or even triple the recipe depending upon the size of the turkey. The dressing used to stuff a turkey should not be as moist as that baked in a casserole because it absorbs moisture from the fowl. Reduce the liquid by one-third.

Dressing in casserole serves 8

Turkey Giblet Gravy

Raw gizzard, neck, heart from turkey or chicken (liver also if desired)
sea salt and freshly ground pepper to taste
1/4   cup minced onion

Cook the giblets about 1½ hours or until tender with the onion and salt and pepper to taste in boiling water. Save the broth. Discard the neck. Chop the gizzard, heart, and liver. Scrape all the good brown solids from the roasting pan of the turkey or chicken. Mix 6 tablespoons of fat from the pan in which the turkey was cooked with 5 tablespoons unbleached flour. Stir until smooth in a skillet. Slowly pour about 2 cups of the giblet cooking liquid into the flour mixture, stirring to avoid lumps from forming. Cook over a low heat. Add the giblets. Continue to stir until thickened.

Makes about 2 cups gravy

Cranberry Relish

Cranberries, like so many of the fruits and vegetables traditionally associated with holiday feasting, were enjoyed first by the Southern Indians.

180

1   lb. cranberries, cooked according to directions on the
    box
1/2   cup homemade applesauce (page 123)
1/4   cup unsulfured raisins
1/4   teaspoon cinnamon

Add all the ingredients together. Chill several hours for flavors to blend. Serve with meat for a change from plain cranberry sauce.

Serves 8

    The sweet smell of cakes rising in the oven as their tops slowly browned leaves its own special memory. Even today the making of the rich fruit cakes must be done, or at least under way, by Thanksgiving or they will not have time to age. Friends and neighbors exchange plates of cakes, cookies, and candies at Christmas time, but Southern cooks specialize in baking cakes. Favorite cakes are fruit cakes, coconut cakes, and pound cakes.

    My mother tells of how she and my daddy used to age the fruit cakes they made: "We usually made our fruit cakes around Thanksgiving time. Some people make them before, but they must be made no later than by Thanksgiving. After they are baked and cooled they are aged. Some people wrapped them in cloths soaked with grape juice for the dark cakes or apple juice for the light ones before the availability of plastic wrap and aluminum foil. Cut up pieces of fresh apple are often put in with the cake before wrapping and sprinkling with juice if they are especially dry. You know, your daddy liked to put booze on them, but I always like them better with the juice instead! We then wrapped them with plastic wrap and then with foil and put them in airtight containers. Check them from time to time to see if they need any more juice. If you want to keep them on past Christmas, they can be kept in the freezer for a year or more. The aging gives the fruits in the cake time to mellow. Their taste improves with the aging."

Mrs. Brunson's Layer Fruit Cake

This is one of our favorites that a Mississippi neighbor used to include in her plate of Christmas goodies that she brought to our house. If you don't care for the heavier type of aged fruit cake, try this. It's a good one!

2   cups white or pulverized raw sugar
1   cup butter or soy margarine
3   fertile eggs
2   teaspoons baking powder
1/4   teaspoon sea salt
grated rind of 1 orange
1   teaspoon pure vanilla extract
3   cups unbleached white flour

Cream the butter and the sugar until light and lemon colored. Add the eggs and beat well. Sift together the flour, salt, and baking powder. Add the flour mixture slowly to the creamed mixture. Mix well. Fold in the grated orange peel and the vanilla. Then add the following:

1   lb. light raisins or dark unsulfured ones
2   cups chopped pecans
1/2   lb. honey-dipped dried cherries (or candied), cut up fine
1/2   lb. honey-dipped dried pineapple (or candied), cut up fine

Bake in 3 layers in a 300 degrees F. oven 45 minutes. Cool and remove from pans. Frost with the LAYER FRUIT CAKE FILLING.

Filling

2   cups pulverized raw sugar
6   tablespoons unbleached white flour
2   fertile eggs, lightly beaten
grated rind of 1 orange
juice of 2 oranges
1   no. 2 can crushed pineapple (if you can't find un-
    sweetened crushed, drain the sliced pineapple that is
    packed in its own juice and crush in blender)
1   cup chopped pecans
1   grated fresh coconut, save some out for sprinkling on
    top of cake

Cook all the above together except nuts and coconut adding
in the order they are listed. Cook until very thick. Add nuts
and coconut after it is cooked. Put the layers together with
filling and put some on top. Sprinkle with coconut.

Serves 10

Coconut Layer Cake

*This is a white cake thickly filled with freshly grated co-
conut between the layers and liberally sprinkled on
top. A cake like this keeps Christmas a happy memory
for many years.*

White Cake

1¾   cups white or pulverized raw sugar
3/4   cup butter or soy margarine
1   cup milk
3   cups unbleached white flour, sifted three times before
      measuring
2   teaspoons baking powder
6   fertile egg whites
1/2   teaspoon pure vanilla extract
1/2 teaspoon pure almond extract
1   grated coconut
Cooked White Frosting

Cream the butter and the sugar until very fluffy. Sift the measured flour and baking powder. Add the sifted flour and baking powder alternatively with the milk. Beat the egg whites until stiff. Fold in the egg whites gently. Add the almond and vanilla extracts. Bake for 25 minutes at 325 degrees F. in two greased and floured 9" cake pans. Cool and remove from the pans. Frost with the COOKED WHITE FROSTING and sprinkle liberally with the freshly grated coconut.

Serves 10–12

Cooked White Frosting

If this is to be a pure white frosting, use the white sugar. Raw sugar, however, gives it only a slight honey color.

2   fertile egg whites
1½   cups white or pulverized raw sugar
1/3   cup water
2   teaspoons corn syrup or light honey
1   teaspoon pure vanilla extract
1/2   teaspoon almond extract

184

Combine the unbeaten egg whites, sugar, water, and corn syrup or honey in the top of a double boiler. Beat until ingredients are well blended. Place over rapidly boiling water and beat with an electric beater until the mixture is light and fluffy and will hold its shape. Remove from the heat. Add the flavorings. Continue to beat the frosting until it is stiff enough to stand up in peaks. Spread between the layers, on top of the cake, and around the sides. Sprinkle coconut between the layers, on top and press onto the icing around the sides.

Frosts 1 cake

Coconut Pound Cake

Grating of fresh coconut is one of the surest signs of holidays to come.

1   stick butter and 2 sticks margarine (all margarine may be used)
3   cups white or pulverized raw sugar
6   fertile eggs
2⅝ cups unbleached white flour or 3 cups cake flour, sifted with salt and soda
1/4 teaspoon sea salt
1/4 teaspoon baking soda
8   ozs. sour cream
1   cup freshly grated coconut
1   teaspoon pure vanilla extract

Preheat the oven to 300 degrees F. Grease and flour a tube pan. Cream the butter and margarine and sugar well. Add the eggs one at a time, mixing well. Add dry ingredients and sour cream. Mix well. Fold in the coconut and vanilla. Bake 1½–2 hours until done.

Makes 1 large cake, serving 10–12

Homemade Candied Fruits for Fruit Cakes and Christmas Cookies

If honey-dipped dried fruits are not available without additives and you want to be sure of what goes into them, here is a recipe.

Whole cherries, apricots, peaches and pears in halves, sliced fresh pineapple, and whole figs can be candied by this method. It is a lengthy and tedious process. It takes slow cooking in installments and having shallow trays for plumping fruit as necessary.

First the fruit to be candied should be washed, peeled or pared if necessary, cut, or sliced and dropped into boiling water for two or three minutes. Drain well. Cover with syrup made by boiling together 1 lb. raw sugar for each lb. of fruit with 1 cup of water. If honey is used substitute 1 lb. natural honey for the raw sugar and change the amount of water to 3/4 cup. Boil rapidly for 15 minutes. Remove from the fire and allow to stand overnight. The next morning boil for 10 or 15 minutes again, and repeat the boiling and cooling for 4 to 6 days according to how rapidly the water is drawn out and the syrup is absorbed. The fruit plumps slowly and the gradual increase in the density of the syrup caused by the many cookings insures tender fruit which is filled with syrup. After the fruit is transparent and bright, lift it from the syrup and dry in the sun or a cool oven.

If crystallized fruit is desired, use fruit prepared by the above recipe. When the fruit is dry, cover it with a heavy syrup and allow it to stand for 2 or 3 days. Then drain off the syrup and dry the pieces of fruit in the sun or in a cool oven.

Dark Fruit Cake

It is not Christmas without fruit cakes. This is a delicious cake packed full of fruits and nuts. The fruits are given as originally written. Honey-dipped dried fruits of your choice or home candied ones may be substituted as long as the total pounds are about the same.

2   cups butter or margarine
2   cups brown sugar
12   fertile egg yolks, well beaten
12   stiffly beaten fertile egg whites
1   cup fruit juice or buttermilk
1/4   cup unsulfured molasses
2   squares of chocolate (or 6 tablespoons carob powder mixed with 4 tablespoons water)
4   cups unbleached white flour
1   teaspoon baking soda
1/2   teaspoon sea salt
2   teaspoons mace
2   teaspoons cloves
2   teaspoons cinnamon
2   teaspoons allspice
1   teaspoon nutmeg
2   pounds unsulfured currants or raisins
4   cups chopped pecans
3   cups chopped unsulfured dates
1   pound crystallized pineapple, sliced thin
1   pound crystallized citron, sliced thin
1/4   pound crystallized orange peel, sliced thin
1/2   pound crystallized lemon peel, sliced thin

Save out 1 cup of flour to dredge the fruits and nuts. Sift the salt and spices with the flour. Dredge the fruits and nuts and add to the flour mixture. Cream the butter and sugar together well. Add the well beaten egg yolks, the fruit juice, molasses, and the chocolate or carob mixture. Gradually add the flour, nuts, and fruit mixture. Put into 2 loaf pans lined with oiled brown paper, smoothing top with a knife.

187

Bake 3 hours in a slow 300 degrees F. oven. When cakes crack on top, they are almost done. Turn over onto the cake racks to cool. When cool wrap them in plastic wrap and then in foil. They will keep for months in an airtight container. They can be frozen for longer periods of time. (See page 181 for aging of fruit cakes).

Makes 2 loaves

Christmas Fruit Bars

1   cup unbleached white flour for dredging fruit
1   teaspoon baking powder
1   cup pulverized raw sugar
4   fertile eggs
1/2 lb. honey-dipped dried or candied cherries
1/2 lb. honey-dipped dried or candied pineapple
1/2 lb. untreated seedless dates
2   cups pecans, chopped
2   tablespoons pineapple juice

Dredge the fruit in flour. To the fruit add the sugar and baking powder. In another bowl beat the eggs and add the juice. Mix all together. Put on a buttered cookie sheet, spreading out over the cookie sheet with a fork. Bake at 275 degrees F. for 1 hour 15 minutes or 1 hour 30 minutes. Cut while hot. Sprinkle with a little more white or pulverized raw sugar. The 1½ pounds of fruit may be any combination of honey-dipped dried fruits available at the health food store or 1½ pounds of home candied fruits.

Makes 18 bars

Christmas Divinity

No Christmas candy assortment is complete without divinity, a Southern favorite. The honey and raw sugar used instead of refined sugar and corn syrup give it an extra good flavor.

2½   cups raw sugar
1/2   cup natural light honey
2/3   cup water
2   egg whites, stiffly beaten
1   cup chopped pecans

Place the sugar, honey, and water in a saucepan. Stir together. Place on to cook. Stir until the sugar dissolves. Then cover the pan for 1 minute. Remove the cover and boil without stirring to 232 degrees F. on the candy thermometer. Have prepared in a mixing bowl the stiffly beaten egg whites. When the candy has reached 232 degrees F., add 1/3 of syrup to the beaten egg whites *very slowly*. Place the candy back on the heat and cook until the syrup forms a hard ball when a small amount is dropped into cold water. The candy thermometer will register about 250 degrees F. Then add the rest of the syrup to the egg whites mixture dripping it in *very slowly* as you mix. This allows the egg and the beaten portion to fluff and become light. Continue beating slowly until the candy becomes firm in the bowl and will hold peaks. At this point add the chopped pecans.

Do not add the nuts until you are sure the candy is ready to be dropped. Fold them in gently by hand. Drop quickly onto greased wax paper. Pecan halves may be pressed into the tops while they are soft if desired. Allow to become firm before moving. Store in airtight container.

Makes 3½ dozen pieces

Brown Sugar Macaroons

1   fertile egg white, slightly beaten
1   cup brown sugar
1   cup finely chopped pecans
1/4   teaspoon sea salt
1   teaspoon pure vanilla extract

Add sugar to beaten egg white. Then add other ingredients. Drop in very small amounts onto a greased cookie sheet and bake in a 350 degrees F. oven until a medium brown color. Cool on the cookie sheet. 1/4 cup grated coconut may be added for variety.

Makes 2 dozen macaroons

Christmas Fruit Cookies

These are delicious fruit cake-like cookies. The candied fruits are now usually store-bought, but honey-dipped dried fruits from the health food store or homemade candied ones may be used.

190

4   fertile eggs
3   cups unbleached white flour or 2 cups unbleached white
     flour and 1 cup whole wheat
1   cup brown sugar
3   teaspoons baking soda
3   tablespoons milk
3/4 cup whiskey or apple juice
1   teaspoon cinnamon
1   teaspoon nutmeg
6   cups shelled pecans, chopped
2   lbs. candied cherries
3   lbs. other candied fruit such as pineapple. Leave fruits
     in chunky pieces, don't cut too fine.
2   lbs. white or unsulfured black raisins soaked in a sweet
     wine or grape juice overnight.

Mix the baking soda with the milk. Mix nuts and fruits
with flour that has been sifted with the cinnamon and nutmeg. Beat the eggs and sugar together well. Add the whiskey and milk and soda mixture to the eggs and sugar. Pour
over the fruit and flour mixture and mix with your hands
until all ingredients are mixed together well. Drop by tea-
spoonfuls onto a greased cookie sheet. Bake in a 350 degrees F. oven for 15–20 minutes.

                                    Makes 5 dozen cookies

Molasses Coconut Chews

*A good candy to box for holiday giving; mixed with
other favorites.*

1/4 cup unsulfured molasses
1   tablespoon cider vinegar
3/4 cup natural honey
2   tablespoons butter or soy margarine
2   cups freshly grated coconut
1   teaspoon pure vanilla extract
pinch of sea salt

Combine molasses, honey, vinegar, and butter. Cook the mixture slowly, stirring occasionally until the mixture forms a soft ball when dropped into cold water (240 degrees F. on the candy thermometer.) Remove and add the coconut, vanilla, and salt. Quickly drop onto a greased surface to cool.

Makes about 24 pieces

Sweet Potato Pone

Sweet potatoes have long been a favorite Southern vegetable. Harnett Kane, a Southern author, tells the story of the desire and longing of a wounded Rebel soldier at Lauderdale Springs, Mississippi, for sweet potato pone for Christmas of 1864. To make it called for potatoes, eggs, and butter—all priceless luxuries. Somehow one of the nurses was able to bargain for and hide the ingredients till Christmas Day 1864 when she made the pone and granted the soldier's wish.

3   cups grated raw sweet potatoes
2   fertile eggs
1/2   cup pulverized raw sugar
1/2   cup dark unsulfured molasses
1/4   cup unbleached white flour
1½   teaspoons nutmeg
1/2   stick butter or soy margarine, melted
1   teaspoon pure vanilla extract

Mix the grated potatoes, sugar, flour, eggs, molasses, nutmeg and vanilla. Pour the melted butter into the mixture and mix well. Pour the mixture into a large cast iron skillet or heavy casserole and bake in a 350 degrees F. oven for 50 minutes.

Serves 6

Czarine Cream

*The old recipe intended this cream to be served as one
of several desserts on a menu. I find this too rich to
serve as a molded dessert, but it makes a tasty topping
for fruit. It was originally colored enough with green
food coloring to tint it delicately.*

1   envelope unflavored gelatin
1/4   cup cold water
1   pint heavy cream
1/3   (or to taste) cup pulverized raw sugar
1   teaspoon pure vanilla extract
1/4   cup finely chopped blanched almonds

Dissolve the gelatin in the water. Beat the cream, adding
the sugar and the vanilla. Mix in the gelatin. Continue beating the cream until thickened. Add the almonds and fold
gently. Place in a mold and put on ice for 1 hour. Unmold
for serving. This will fill 4 small molds or one 2 cup mold. If
it is to be used as a topping, just refrigerate for an hour or
two before using.

Serves 4 as a molded dessert

In some parts of the South the slaves were given a holiday from all work at Christmas time and were paid for
their work as long as the yule log still burned. A typical
Christmas dinner for the slaves in Virginia might have con-
sisted of pork pie, 'possum, yams or a stuffed 'coon (rac-
coon) basted with molasses. 'Possums and 'coons are still
considered good eating by some people, both black and
white. The 'possums are chased down by dogs and taken
back and kept in a pen for a while and fed before killing
them. Other people consider the 'possum less than a clean
animal since it will eat anything and prefer instead the
more particular 'coon which carefully cleans everything it
eats. Both animals are cooked whole, head and all. A baked
sweet potato is stuck into its mouth as a garnish.

Roast 'Possum

'Possum is a very fat peculiarly flavored meat.

First catch the 'possum. Clean it thoroughly. Soak it in salted water for 12 hours, more or less, depending upon the size and the age of the 'possum. The larger older ones will take a longer soaking time. After it is soaked, parboil it in salted water for 30 minutes. Mix together:

3   cups bread crumbs
1   chopped onion
1/4   cup fresh chopped parsley
sea salt and freshly ground pepper to taste
'possum liver, chopped fine
1   beaten fertile egg

Stuff the 'possum with this mixture. Sew it up. Place in a baking pan with just a little water. Place in a 425 degrees F. oven for 15–20 minutes. Pour off the juice and keep. Lay partially boiled sweet potatoes around the 'possum. Lay slices of bacon across the 'possum and potatoes to keep from drying out. Pour the juice back over both and let bake another hour or more depending on the size of the 'possum, basting frequently. When done take up on a platter and garnish with sprigs of parsley and sliced lemon. Put a baked apple or sweet potato in its mouth.

Number of servings depends on size of 'possum. Average 'possum serves 4.

Oyster a la Creole

2   pints oysters
1   lb. fresh okra, cut up
6   green onions, chopped fine
1   large sweet green pepper, chopped fine
5   celery stalks, chopped fine
1   (8 oz.) can tomato sauce
2   cups beef bouillon
2   cups water
2   tablespoons cider vinegar
1   tablespoon sea salt
1   tablespoon raw sugar
1   stick margarine or butter

Finely chop the vegetables. Brown lightly in melted margarine. When golden brown, add the tomato sauce, beef bouillon, water, and seasonings. Simmer over low heat for 1 hour. Add the oysters and continue cooking until the oysters are plump and the edges ruffled. Serve as an appetizer or as a main course.

Serves 4 as a main course
Serves 6–8 as an appetizer

A SOUTHERN CHRISTMAS DINNER

This is one of the simpler Christmas dinner menus from an old Southern cookbook written about 1900 belonging to my great-aunt.

Oyster Cocktail   *Bread Sticks*
Oysters à la Creole (page 195)   *Bouillon Supreme*
Radishes   *Olives*
Celery
Roast Turkey (page 178)   *Giblet Sauce (page 180)*
Bread Stuffing (page 179)
Cranberry Relish (page 180)
Orange Sherbet
Roast Wild Duck   *Celery and Apple Salad*
Czarine Cream (page 193)   *Angel Cream Cake*
Confectionery
Café Noir

From the *Good Housekeeper's Cook Book*, written in 1908, comes a different Christmas menu, traditionally English in its main features. The entire cost of the meal for *6 persons was five dollars!*

Grape Fruit or Oyster Canapés
Pickled Pears (home made)   *Celery*
Oxtail or Mock Turtle Soup
Roast Green Goose with Apple Sauce, or Roast Sirloin of Beef with Browned Potatoes and Yorkshire Pudding
Mashed Irish Potatoes or Baked Sweet Potatoes
Boiled Onions with Cream Sauce
Roman Punch (homemade)
Roast Pigeons   *Orange and Endive Salad*
Pippins and Cheese
Plum Pudding with Brandy Sauce
Syllabub   *Nuts*   *Raisins*
Coffee (demitasse)

New Year's Eve comes after several weeks of seasonal festivities. The house is still decorated with magnolia leaves in addition to the usual holly and mistletoe. Now is the time for a relaxed welcoming of the New Year. Southerners associate "good luck" in the coming year with the eating of black-eyed peas cooked with hog jowl on New Year's Day. A late New Year's Eve supper might be:

Hog Jowl and Black-Eyed Peas (page 56 and Page 197)
Pig Feet, Ears, and Tails (page 197)
Baked Ham and Beaten Biscuits (pages 85 and 23)
Rice   Turnip Greens (page 49)
Corn bread (page 14)
Fruit Cake (page 182)
Buttermilk   Beer

The pig feet, ears, and tails give an extra share of good luck to those who can eat them. The ham is offered for those who cannot. The rice may be mixed with the black-eyed peas to make Hopping John.

New Year's Pig Feet, Ears, and Tails

Simmer about 4 lbs. of fresh pig's feet, ears, and tails in a large pot with sea salt, freshly ground pepper, and a little vinegar to taste. Simmer until the bones fall out.

Serves 8

Hog Jowl and Black-Eyed Peas

Some folks believe that black-eyed peas must be the first thing that they put into their mouths on New Year's Day. Long cooking is the secret to good-tasting hog jowl, a dish first famous before the War Between the States. The dish eaten now on New Year's Day with corn bread originated in the slaves' Christmas meal.

1   lb. dried black-eyed peas, washed and soaked in water
    overnight
1   lb. hog jowl

Cook the hog jowl in salted water in a pot until nearly
tender. Add the peas and soaking liquid. Cook in the pot
until the peas are tender.

Serves 8

Nothing compares with Christmas, but the next most important holiday would be Easter followed by Thanksgiving,
New Year's Eve, the Fourth of July, and then special local
celebrations. Easter in some areas is begun by a sunrise service at a large outdoor gathering place where the resurrection
of Christ is celebrated as the Easter Day dawns. When Easter
services are over, when all the new outfits have been admired, and all the Easter eggs hunted down, thoughts turn
to food. Ham is a popular main dish for the Easter meal.
Thanksgiving is celebrated with a large dinner, but the emphasis on family gatherings is not quite as great as it is at
Christmas and Easter.

Glazed Easter Ham

*See pages 81–83 for information on hams. Whichever
ham you choose this method of glazing may be used.
Hams are too often glazed and garnished with cloves
and pineapple slices. This is a pretty tulip-red change.*

10   lb. ham
24   long stemmed cloves
1/2   cup brown sugar
2   cups thick cold freshly made cranberry relish (page 181)

Choose the type of ham you prefer and bake according to
directions. One half hour before the end of the baking time,

remove the ham from the oven. Score the fat with a sharp knife into diamond shapes. Stud with cloves. Return the ham to the baking pan, pouring off first any fat that has collected in the bottom of the pan. Mix the cranberry sauce and brown sugar. Spread over the ham and bake 30 minutes more, basting occasionally with sauce if needed. Spoon the hot cranberry sauce from the bottom of the pan over the ham just before serving. This is enough glaze for about a 10 lb. ham.

> 10 lb. ham serves 20
> depending upon the
> amount of fat and bone

Maggie's Holiday Dressing

This rice dressing recipe belongs to a favorite cousin who serves this with smoked turkeys and hams Thanksgiving, Christmas, or Easter. It's fine enough for the nicest dinner and a change from the usual corn bread dressing.

2   cups brown rice (or mixed white and wild rice)
1   large chopped onion
4   large stalks celery, chopped
1   green sweet pepper, chopped
1   cup chopped chicken or turkey gizzards (cook gizzards in salted water until tender before chopping)
1/2   cup butter or soy margarine
1   tablespoon sea salt
1   tablespoon poultry seasoning
2   fertile eggs
1   cup chopped pecans
1/2   cup chopped fresh parsley
1   pint oysters
1/2   cup chopped fresh mushrooms

Cook rice according to the directions on the package. While the rice is cooking, sauté the onion, celery, pepper, and giz-

199

zards in the butter until thoroughly cooked. Add the seasonings and mix. Beat the eggs until frothy. Remove sautéed onion mixture from the heat. Add the cooked rice and fold into the beaten eggs, mixing thoroughly. Add the chopped nuts and parsley. Add the oysters and mushrooms. Stuff turkey for the last 30 minutes of its cooking time or bake in a buttered casserole 25 minutes in a preheated 350 degrees F. oven.

Serves 6

Mrs. Adam's Thanksgiving Pumpkin Pie

A Mississippi neighbor's recipe for an easy pumpkin pie good enough for any meal's dessert.

1   cup pulverized raw sugar
1   cup milk
1   cup cooked pumpkin
1   teaspoon pure vanilla extract
1   tablespoon unbleached flour or 1 teaspoon arrowroot
unbaked 9" pie shell

Put all ingredients into a bowl and mix well. Pour into an unbaked pie shell. Bake at 350 degrees F. until done, about 45–50 minutes. Custard will be set and the top browned. The center may look a little soft. It will set later. Cooking a pumpkin pie too long makes it watery.

Serves 6

The Fourth of July is usually celebrated with lots of fireworks and family picnics. The picnic menu would include fried chicken, biscuits, potato salad, relishes, pies, cakes, iced tea, and watermelon. Following the meal and a rest in the shade from the heat there would perhaps be a game of softball for all. There are some public fireworks displays, but each family usually does its own. Fireworks are supposedly banned in some areas, but they can usually be found for sale outside the city limits. Fireworks have traditionally been very much a part of the Southern celebration of Christmas, New Year's Eve, and the 4th of July.

There are some celebrations that are peculiar to the South. Memorial Day for Confederate soldiers precedes the National Memorial Day. Mississippi celebrates it the 4th Monday in April. At this time groups such as the United Daughters of the Confederacy mark Confederate graves with little Confederate flags and flowers. Often great buckets of flowers are left at the graves, fresh reminders that this is still *the* war in the hearts of proud Southerners. There are no special foods associated with this occasion, but what would be more appropriate than an informal coffee afterwards at which Robert E. Lee Cake or Jefferson Davis Pie is served in commemoration?

The first celebration of Robert E. Lee's birthday as a legal holiday was in Georgia in 1889. His birthday is casually observed in most Southern states, but the main observance today is at Washington and Lee University at Lexington, Virginia, where his memory is faithfully revered.

Jefferson Davis' birthday is remembered in most Southern states and in some coincides with the Confederate Memorial Day celebrations which vary from local picnics and speeches to the traditional graveside tributes to the Confederate dead.

Jefferson Davis Pie

This is one of the many "Famous Name" desserts. The Jefferson Davis Pie was originated by Aunt Jule Ann, a slave in the family of George B. Warren of Missouri. The family moved there from the South before the War Between the States. Aunt Jule Ann admired Jefferson Davis and named this pie after him when she first made it for distinguished guests in Missouri.

2 cups white or pulverized raw sugar
1 tablespoon unbleached white flour
1 cup cream
1 cup butter or soy margarine
6 fertile eggs, separated and 3 more egg whites for meringue
1 unbaked 9" pie shell

Cream the butter and sugar together well. Add the flour and cream and beat all until light and frothy. Add the egg yolks one at a time, mixing well. Beat the egg whites until stiff. Fold them into the pie mixture gently. Pour into an unbaked pie shell. Bake at 400 degrees F. about 40 minutes as you would for a custard. It is done when the pie is set and a knife inserted comes out clean. Beat the other 3 egg whites until stiff, adding sugar to taste. Put onto top of done pie and put pie back into the oven to brown the meringue.

Serves 6

Robert E. Lee Cake

The original cake named in honor of Robert E. Lee called for 12 eggs, their full weight in sugar, and half their weight in flour. This is one of the best known historical "Famous Name" cakes.

9 fertile egg yolks, beaten
9 fertile egg whites, stiffly beaten
2 cups white or pulverized raw sugar
2 cups unbleached flour
1/2 teaspoon sea salt
1 teaspoon freshly squeezed lemon juice
1 teaspoon freshly squeezed orange juice
grated rind of 1 lemon

Beat the egg yolks very lightly and slowly. Add in the sugar and beat well. Add the fruit juices and rind. Fold in the well beaten egg whites. Sift the flour with the salt and mix gently into the batter. Pour into 3 ungreased layer pans and bake at 300 degrees F. for about 30 minutes until done. Cool and ice with ROBERT E. LEE FROSTING.

Robert E. Lee Frosting

3   cups white or pulverized raw sugar
1/2   cup freshly squeezed orange juice
1/2   cup water
3   egg whites, stiffly beaten
grated rind of 1 lemon
1   tablespoon lemon juice
1   cup freshly grated coconut

Boil the sugar, water and orange juice until syrup spins a thread. Pour into the whites of the eggs very slowly, stirring constantly. Add lemon juice and grated lemon rind to icing. Spread between layers and on top and sides. Sprinkle with grated coconut.

Makes 1 large cake
Serves 12

MENUS

If you've never eaten in the South, I know you're probably asking "What goes with what?" The menu patterns given here will help you work out your own combinations to include the following groups:

MENU PATTERN I

Breakfast	*Dinner*	*Supper*
fruit	protein dish	main dish
cereal	starch food	bread
bread	2 other vegetables	salad or dessert
protein dish	bread	beverage
beverage	salad	
	dessert	
	beverage	

MENU PATTERN II

Breakfast	*Lunch or Supper*
fruit juice (citrus or toma-to)	main dish, soup, or sand-wich
protein food (meat and/or eggs)	1 vegetable and/or salad
bread or cereal	bread, butter or margarine
beverage	dessert (optional)
	beverage

Dinner
Main dish
starchy food
green and/or yellow vegetable
salad
bread, butter or margarine
beverage

You must be asking by now "Do they really eat all that?" *Yes,* they do. It is a well-balanced diet. The trick is to eat small portions. I know, since I've never weighed over 105 pounds and I've always eaten like that.

SAMPLE MENUS FOR DINNER OR
SPECIAL SUPPERS

CREAMED OYSTERS (PAGE 178)

ROAST CHICKEN   DRESSING (PAGE 179)

GREEN BEANS (PAGE 51)   SQUASH CASSEROLE (PAGE 61)

FROZEN FRUIT SALAD

HOMEMADE ROLLS (PAGE 27)   BUTTER

PECAN PIE (PAGE 152)

ICED TEA AND COFFEE (MILK FOR CHILDREN) (PAGE 164)

RELISH PLATE

CRAB MEAT IN PATTY SHELLS (PAGE 97)

VIRGINIA HAM (PAGE 84)   BEATEN BISCUITS (PAGE 23)

SCALLOPED POTATOES (PAGE 60)   GREENS (PAGE 48)

BLACK BOTTOM PIE (PAGE 144)

ICED TEA AND COFFEE (PAGE 164)

BIBLIOGRAPHY

Clark, Linda, *Stay Young Longer*, New York: Pyramid, 1968.

Barrett, James H., *The American Christmas*, New York: The Macmillan Company, 1968.

Botkin, B. A., *A Treasury of Southern Folklore*, New York: Crown Publishers, 1949.

—————————, *Lay My Burden Down*, Chicago, Illinois: The University of Chicago Press, 1945.

Drury, John, *Rare and Well Done*, Chicago, Illinois: Quadrangle Books, 1966.

Kainer, Ruth Cole, *America's Christmas Heritage*, New York: Funk and Wagnalls, 1969.

Kane, Harnett T., *Gone Are the Days*, New York: E. P. Dutton, 1960.

—————————, *The Southern Christmas Book*, New York: David McKay, 1958.

—————————, *Deep Delta Country*, New York: American Folkways Series, 1944.

——————————, *The Romantic South,* New York: Coward-Mc-Cann, 1961.

Levitt, Eleanor, *The Wonderful World of National Food Cookery,* Great Neck, New York: Hearthside Press 1971.

Lewis, Taylor Biggs, Jr. and Joane Young, *Christmas in Williamsburg,* N.Y.: Holt, Rinehart and Winston, Inc., 1970.

McClure, Jon A., *Meat Eaters Are Threatened,* New York: Pyramid, 1973.

Myers, Robert J., *Celebrations—The Complete Book of American Holidays,* Garden City, New York: Doubleday and Company, Inc., 1972.

Norris, P. E., *About Molasses,* New York: Pyramid, 1972.

Rodale, J. I. and Staff, *The Organic Directory,* Emmaus, Pa.: Rodale Press Books, 1971.

Rouse, Parke Jr., *Below the James Lies Dixie,* Richmond, Virginia: The Dietz Press, 1968.

Warmbrand, Max, *Eat Well to Keep Well,* New York: Pyramid, 1970.

INDEX

209